THE EXCHANGED LIFE

THE REVELATION OF JESUS CHRIST IN YOU

RHONDA J. MEAD

ISBN 978-1-64258-407-3 (paperback)
ISBN 978-1-64258-408-0 (digital)

Christian Faith Publishing, Inc.
832 Park Avenue
Meadville, PA 16335
www.christianfaithpublishing.com

Scriptures, unless otherwise noted, taken from "the NEW AMERICAN STANDARD BIBLE(R)," Copyright(C) 1960, 1962, 1963, 1968, 1971, 1972, 1973, 1975, 1977, 1995 by The Lockman Foundation. Used by permission.

Printed in the United States of America

Contents

Acknowledgments

First Edition:

To Shelley who urged me to write down what the Lord had taught me.

To Suzanne who, before I discovered the computer, suffered through my longhand to type the original text.

To Steve and Lisa for their editing and layout of the first edition.

To my family for their willingness to share my time, so I could share with you.

And, of course, to my Heavenly Father, who gave me a reason to write.

This Edition:

For the testimonies of the precious souls whose lives were changed by the first edition.

To our prayer team: for their prayers, encouragement and faithful friendship. They are as excited about this publication as I am!

To my husband, Richard, for his loving gift of the time needed to prepare this manuscript and for his deeply-held belief in the necessity for the message in this book to be available in print.

Specifically, to our daughter Amber. Along with being a member of our prayer team, she has been my literary coach, consultant, editor, and publicist. She has patiently given endless hours toward the production of this book.

Introduction

There is more to your Christian walk than you are experiencing! If you know your Christian life is not fulfilling and realistically is far different in experience than what is found in the Bible, you need to keep reading. Every Christian's life should be a revelation of the life of Christ within them, but sadly enough, few believe deep down this is a reality. Surrender, commitment, and Christian service are not the answers in and of themselves and may have left you disenchanted, never having found the peace and joy the Bible speaks so freely of.

In order to experience true fulfillment, we must achieve God's intent for each and every believer, which is to be conformed to the image of Christ. This is the only way the world will see Jesus. Jesus, Himself, said, "And I, if I am lifted up from the earth, will draw all men to Myself" (John 12:32). Mature sons and daughters are God's plan for the revelation of His Son to a lost world. This plan will not only allow the world to see Jesus, but will give the peace, joy, and fulfillment so many are desperately seeking.

Our goal must be to allow the life of Christ to permeate every part of us—spirit, soul, and body. As we yield to the Spirit, "the life of Jesus" will "be manifested in our body" (II Corinthians 4:11). This is the process of the revelation of Jesus Christ in you. What is on the inside will be seen on the outside—not through will power—but step by step, moment by moment, through the choices we make. The Apostle Paul made the goal clear to the Galatians, who had fallen back to ritual and fleshly observances. He used the analogy of a woman in labor, ready to give birth. He then declared to the Galatians that he, too, would continue in "labor until Christ is formed in you" (Galatians 4:19).

The late Ian Thomas stated this so succinctly. His summary of the purpose for our existence on this earth was for us to "become the visible representation of the invisible God."

> Always carrying about in the body the dying of Jesus, that the life of Jesus also may be manifested in our body. For we who live are constantly being delivered over to death for Jesus sake, that the life of Jesus also may be manifested in our mortal flesh. (II Corinthians 4:10–11)

> And we know that God causes all things to work together for good to those who love God, to those who are called according to His purpose. For whom He foreknew, He also predestined to become conformed to the image of His Son, that He might be the firstborn among many brethren. (Romans 8:28–29)

Preface

Many years ago, the truths of The Exchanged Life changed my life forever. The Lord lovingly showed me the answer to my every need through the revelation of what the life of Christ, released in my life, could do. Let me share my story—without any exaggeration and with all humility.

I was raised in a "church going" family. We went to church most Sundays and participated in the social life of the church. Although our church did not clearly teach the need for a personal relationship with Jesus Christ, I am thankful that as a result of many years of Sunday School, I have loved Jesus as long as I can remember.

When I was twelve years of age, my brother, who was thirteen years older than me, received Christ as his Savior while away at college. When he came home for the summer, he brought me to a local evangelical church and I gladly received Christ—Whom I already loved—as my Lord and Savior.

It is important to understand the difference the exchanged life can make in the life of the "best" Christian. As soon as I was old enough to go to the evangelical church by myself (when my brother was away at college), I plunged myself into to the activities of the church—not out of duty, but because I loved the activities and I loved the Lord with all my heart! I started teaching Sunday School at age sixteen, participated in evangelistic campaigns, went on weekly door-to-door visitation, ran Junior Church, filled in for nursery, made the bulletin, and did anything else needing done. During this time, I had a diligent devotional and prayer life, and the motive of my heart in service was pure. After getting married and having children, my church duties matured, but my passion for the Lord never changed. I was still not trying to earn anything from God, and I clearly understood and embraced His grace and forgiveness.

Just in case you're thinking my problem was I hadn't totally surrendered to Christ, every time we had an evangelist come to speak and challenged us to "remove self from the throne of our life and put Christ in His rightful place," I did, and I meant it with all my heart. The Lord knew I was serious about my love and commitment to Him, so He graciously allowed circumstances to come into my life that brought me to the place where my heart had always wanted to be.

I went from being the person my friends would describe as one "who could do anything she sets her mind to" to being in a position of having such emotional pain that I continually begged the Lord to end my life (since, as a Christian, I could not take my own). The pain was unbearable; my hands shook continuously from my nervous condition, and I took Valium at night in order to get some sleep. Still, when I opened my eyes the next morning, the truth that "the nightmare was real" was always there.

My pastor, at the time, sent me to a ministry called "Life Center." He himself had not experienced The Exchanged Life but was faithfully led by God to direct me to the place with the answer I needed.

As I sat in one of Life Center's offices, shaking miserably on the other side of the "counselor's" desk, I listened to scriptures I knew well, but to a truth I had never grasped. I really did not understand the difference between what I had already done and what was being shared with me. However, God, in His mercy, after two hours of listening to the counselor teach the scriptures, moved me to pray the prayer he asked me to pray. We know it is never about the prayer we pray, but is always about the condition of our hearts. I told the counselor that day, "I don't understand, but I am so miserable I will try anything." After years of ministry, I myself would not have great hopes for freedom for a person who would pray like that. Nonetheless, on that day, God gave His daughter—who really loved Him, but sincerely did not understand—*freedom*! I have never been the same again.

This is why this book needed to be written. If "one of the best, most sincere" Christians was in this state, with no spiritual answer, there is something we are missing in the Body of Christ. The Exchanged Life is not a new teaching; it is a core truth of scripture that has fallen by the wayside through years of church evolution. Some may talk about it, but few have experienced it and many teach the truths without sharing the absolute necessity it is for the Christian life. It is not just an answer to those in crisis, but is a necessary step in the spiritual life of every sincere believer!

CHAPTER 1

Confidence in God

Why is the church of Christ, the very body of the living Lord, virtually powerless in turning this world upside down? There are revivals stirring in other parts of the world. We have moments of intense manifestations of the Holy Spirit in America, but by and large, Jesus is not seen.

We do not see the power of God in our everyday lives because we have not placed our confidence in Him. There is more to confidence than just acknowledging the Lord's presence in our midst. In order for confidence in God to have its perfect work, we must have come to the end of trusting any other person or thing.

One of the greatest reasons for the power of God not being seen in America is our affluence. It is very difficult to have no confidence in anyone or anything but God, when there are so many other options available. If you are without a job, there is unemployment. When your unemployment runs out, there is government assistance. If your employment ends because of illness, there are workman's compensation and disability benefits. Not that any of these are wrong in themselves, but there are so many means of escape besides God. Few turn to God as their sole source of deliverance, because so many other ways exist. There are so many things for our confidence to be in that even if we are praying and "trusting" God, the bottom line is our trust is not in Him alone. Consequently, where we are double minded regarding the source of our hope for deliverance, there is little power.

Even with our affluence, and the many options available, we could still follow our heart's leading in order to wait upon the Lord. Yet for us to be obedient to the prompting of our hearts, we will usually have to undergo discomfort. When we are unwilling to undergo discomfort in order to see the power of God manifested in our lives, we will seldom see the deliverance that the saints of old experienced. When we experience divine deliverance in our lives, our faith is strengthened and we have great confidence in God, not only in His ability to deliver us but in His desire to move mightily in our lives. Our Father is "always ready to help in times of trouble" (Psalm 46:1 NLT), but we seldom wait long enough to see His solution. We do not see miracles and answers that are greater than we could ever ask or think, because we do not, "wait for the Lord" (Isaiah 40:31). The word *wait* in Isaiah 40:31 means to depend on without an alternate plan. When we do wait only on God as our source of hope, we are promised that we will "run and not get tired ...walk and not become weary" (Isaiah 40:31). The problem is few wait for the Lord. In order to wait, we must have no confidence in anything or anyone else besides God and must be determined to rest in our confidence of His eventual deliverance. When we do, we will see divine intervention in our lives that will not only deliver us out of our plight but will also strengthen our trust in God. It has often been said that if we never had anything to be delivered out of, we would not know God as our deliverer. If we never had a need, we would not know Him as our provider. If we were never sick, we would not know Him as our healer.

The process, then, is to have a great need in our life or great lack in our character. Then to remain in that situation long enough to know that there is no way we can change ourselves or change the situation we find ourselves in. Finally, we must not take or make an avenue of escape other than God's deliverance. If we will depend only on Him, we will see the power of God move in our lives, and we will have greater and greater confidence in Him.

Our lack of confidence in God's ability to set us free from any situation or any personal bondage is especially true in the case of mental health. We might be able to accept that God will always provide for our material needs, we might believe that He is our healer and be willing to endure great physical pain, we may understand the power of the life of our risen Savior within us to change our character into His image and be able to wait for Him to perfect that which concerns us; but presented with an emotional or mental problem in ourselves or others, we will usually run to someone with "credentials."

What credentials did Jesus have? He was born in a manger and raised as a carpenter, with only a small amount of schooling. Yet when the man possessed by Legion stood before Jesus, He trusted in the One who had sent Him, and the man from Gerasenes left clothed and in his right mind. Remember, Jesus came to earth and lived as a man, filled with Holy Spirit, totally dependent on the Father, to show us how we should and can walk.

Believing that Jesus is the answer to every mental, emotional, or physical need we will ever have seems like a radical stand, but the scripture clearly teaches this perspective. There are Christian professionals who are trained in psychotherapy and psychiatry, but the scripture does not say the power of God is in the training of men. It says:

> The word of the cross…is the power of God, and the
> foolishness of God is wiser than men and the weakness
> of God is stronger than men. (I Corinthians 1:25)

Who or what is your confidence in?

Christian counseling professionals are trained with material derived from humanistic secular psychology. There is no biblical curriculum for psychotherapy. The very root of the word psychotherapy, that being "psycho," refers to the soul, the area of the personality—the realm of the mind, will, and emotions. The curriculum that we Christians derive from the world teaches us how to deal with the soul of man. Consequently, well-meaning Christian professionals are taught, even in Christian colleges to deal with the soul. The diagnosed emotional and mental health problems manifest themselves in the realm of the soul, but these are only the symptoms of the real problem—"self" in control of the life, instead of Christ.

Most Christians do not have confidence in the power of the cross, because they do not understand what happened to them when they were born again. When we accepted Jesus as our savior, we were "baptized into Christ Jesus" (Romans 6:3). This means that we were immersed into His life. Christ's life has no beginning, and it will never end. There is also no time element in the spirit. So once we are in Christ, it is as though we were always in Him. Our mortal minds which are programmed to time cannot understand what scripture clearly teaches as reality. In other words, we were in Christ when He was crucified, when He was buried, when He defeated the forces of hell, and when He rose again and sat down at the right hand of the Father.

This is the "word of the cross" that the "perishing" do not understand. Regretfully, the perishing can also include believers who have not identified with Christ in His death. We can be destined to spend eternity with God and still not be experiencing the kingdom of heaven on this earth. God's kingdom is life. Satan's kingdom is death. We can be citizens of the kingdom of God and not be experiencing much more of abundant life than unbelievers who belong to Satan's kingdom. We must live according to kingdom principles in order to experience God's will on earth as it is in heaven. When we live by kingdom principles and identify with Christ in His death, burial, and resurrection, we will know that the "word of the cross" is definitely the power of God.

We have let our lack of confidence and understanding of what "Christ in us" really means compel us to run to those who depend on scripture mixed with secular psychology or to send others to brothers and sisters who are well meaning, but are not depending on the "word of the cross" as the sole means of deliverance. We run to other sources besides Jesus because we have no confidence in the Christ who lives in us. We are so self-centered, prone to introspection, and busy looking at the frailty of our flesh that we forget to look at "Christ who is our life," as our "strength."

> When Christ, who is our life, is revealed, then you also will be revealed with Him in glory. (Colossians 3:4)

> I can do all things through Him who strengthens me. (Philippians 4:13)

If we are depending on our performance as the basis for our confidence, then we will continue to be a powerless body, because we are not depending on the strength and character of our head, Jesus Christ.

All through scripture, God constantly warns of mixture. When will the church of Jesus Christ realize that Jesus is the only answer? He is the only answer for every physical, emotional, and material need we will ever have. He is the answer as the written word, giving us guidelines for kingdom living, or as the word that dwells within us, giving us all we need for life and godliness.

When we make choices in our life, only according to what is comfortable or what seems right to those around us, we most likely will reap a decline in the quality of our life. Also, if we choose to deal with our soulish symptoms, rather than seeking the root of our problems, which is always spiritual, we will receive only temporary relief. Jesus died that we might be "free indeed," which is absolutely free. If we settle for anything less, we are letting our flesh or the enemy rob us of the abundant life that Jesus died to give us.

> If therefore the Son shall make you free, you shall be
> free indeed. (John 8:36)

Either the church of Jesus Christ is missing significant keys to kingdom living or God is a liar. The early church turned the world upside down because they possessed an understanding of their inheritance in Christ that the modern church does not understand. They also had a confidence in the power of God, gained through trials and tribulation that the affluent church of America does not possess.

The following pages shall attempt to bring forth how to walk with the Spirit of Christ in control of our lives. When He is in control, we will be ruled by our spirits rather than our souls. When the Spirit of Christ is in control of the soul, then His attributes will be seen in the mind, will, and emotions. These truths will not only set you free but give you the divine confidence to lead others into freedom also. As we proceed in our understanding of the "exchanged life," remember this precept: if you have little confidence in God, you will experience little of the power of God in your life!

Personal Study

1. In your own words, paraphrase I Corinthians 1: 18–31.
    Only as you renew your mind to the truth of scripture will you
    realize how much you have been programmed by the world.

    ____

    ____

    ____

2. Do you really act like you believe what God's word says about
    the wisdom of men?

    ____

    ____

    ____

3. In your own words, paraphrase John 8:31–36.

    ____

    ____

    ____

4. What is truth to you?
    What do you proclaim truth to be to others? In what areas do
    you rationalize? Compromise?

    ____

    ____

    ____

CHAPTER 2

Man: Spirit, Soul, and Body

What is the makeup of man? The vast majority of Christians, let alone the general population, have no idea of the three parts of man, and those who do usually have very little understanding of their function.

In order to understand the war that sometimes rages within us, we need to understand who is fighting. We need to know how we are made and who we really are. Who we really are is spirit, which is encased in a soul, which is encased in a body.

Diagram 2.1

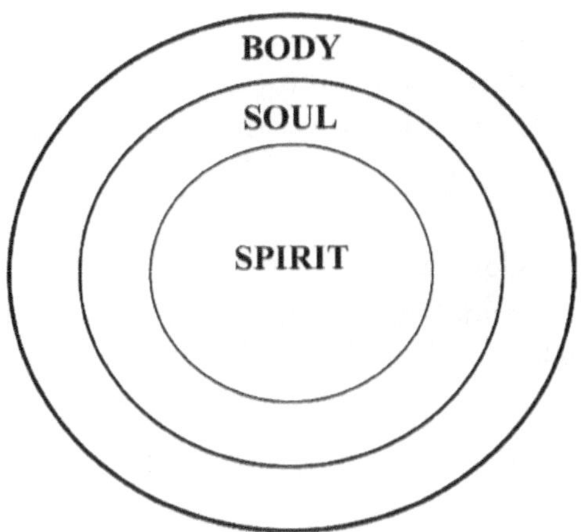

Before you were born again, your spirit was dead to God. When you received Christ as your Savior your spirit was made alive.

> And if Christ is in you, though the body is dead because of sin, yet the spirit is alive because of righteousness. (Romans 8:10)

In other words, you could not communicate, as in fellowship, with God (we will not get into whether or not God hears the prayers of the unregenerate, other than the prayer of salvation. When we get home, you can ask Him). Your unregenerate human spirit had a force of its own in ruling your life. It also could easily be affected by demonic forces. It was incapable of righteousness.

> For all of us have become like one who is unclean,
> And all our righteous deeds are like a filthy garment;
> And all of us wither like a leaf, And our iniquities, like
> the wind, take us away. (Isaiah 64:6)

When you received Jesus as your Savior, you were born again, and the Holy Spirit joined your human spirit, no longer separable, but still both existing in essence. For our mortal minds, I use this example. If you pour a glass of cola into a glass of orange soda, you no longer have cola, nor do you have orange, but they are both there. Now, your spirit man is the temple of the Holy Spirit, sometimes referred to as the Spirit of Christ or the Spirit of the Father. They are one Spirit.

> And the glory[1] which Thou hast given Me I have given to them; that they may be one, Just as We are one. (John 17:22)

Since your human spirit is joined to God's Spirit, your human spirit is seated at the right hand of the Father, in Christ Jesus.

---

[1] "glory" meaning essence–one in essence. Vine's Expository Dictionary

> And raised us up with Him, and seated us with Him
> in the heavenly places, in Christ Jesus. (Ephesians 2:6)

There are no boundaries or distance in the spirit. Don't try to figure it out with your mortal mind!

In this born-again condition, you now *have a choice* to yield to righteousness or unrighteousness.

> And do not go on presenting the members of your
> body to sin as instruments of unrighteousness; but
> present yourselves to God as those alive from the
> dead, and your members as instruments of righteous-
> ness to God. (Romans 6:13)

Now, back to the soul; your soul consists of your mind, will, and emotions. This is the area of your personality. Your soul is basically neutral. I like to think of it as the adapter that transforms the power of the spirit (evil, human, or holy), for use in this earthly realm. To function adequately on this earth, a spirit needs a soul for expression, such as thoughts, choices or feelings, and a body for sense consciousness—taste, sight, touch, smell, and hearing. Just imagine the "Twilight Zone" effect of a spirit floating around by itself with no source of communication or function apart from spirit to spirit. That might be all right for communication with God or evil spirits, but we wouldn't be very effective in reaching the lost. That is one reason why Jesus sent the Comforter to abide in us so that God would still be in the flesh, our flesh—body and soul. So a lost and dying world could still see and relate to Him. Some days it's a scary thought that all that is left on this earth for them to see is us!

Although, the soul is neutral in itself, there is another force, other than the spirit, that fights for control of the soul and the body. The bible calls this force the "flesh" or "self." What is this vague term that everyone talks about but few understand?

To explain the "flesh," which is synonymous with "self," we must again understand what happened when we were born again. Our old nature, "old man" (Romans 6:6 KJV) was crucified with Christ.

> Knowing this, that our old self was crucified with Him,
> that our body of sin might be done away with, that we
> should no longer be slaves to sin. (Romans 6:6)

When Jesus died, your old nature died with Him. When He rose from the dead, He became your new nature. How did this happen? This is the mystery of the gospel! Again, we are working with the limitation of the mortal mind, but remember Christ's life has no beginning and it has no end. It is *eternal life.*

> And He is the image of the invisible God, the first-born of all creation. For by Him all things were created, both in the heavens and on earth, visible and invisible, whether thrones or dominions or rulers or authorities–all things have been created by Him and for Him. And He is before all things, and in Him all things hold together. (Colossians 1:15–17)

> Jesus Christ is the same yesterday and today, and forever. (Hebrews 13:8)

When you receive Christ as Savior you are "in Him."

> Just as He chose us in Him before the foundation of the world, that we should be holy and blameless before Him, in love. (Ephesians 1:4)

> That they may all be one; even as Thou, Father, art in Me, and I in Thee, that they also may be in us; that the world may believe that Thou didst send Me. (John 17:21)

Once Christ becomes your life, you and He possess the same life, or nature.

> When Christ, who is our life, is revealed, then you also
> will be revealed with Him in glory. (Colossians 3:4)

> For by these He has granted to us His precious and
> magnificent promises, in order that by them you
> might become partakers of the divine nature, having
> escaped the corruption that is in the world by lust.
> (II Peter 1:4)

Since His life has no beginning or end, neither do ours (in the spirit). So at any given point in His life, we are in Him including when He died, when He was buried, when He defeated the forces of hell, and when He was resurrected. We are now sitting with Him at the right hand of the Father. Let me try to come up with a poor earthly analogy of a mighty spiritual truth. If I had a river of life, with no beginning or end, and I placed a drop of water in it, where along the river is the drop? You're right! The drop of water, being the same essence as the river, is now part of the river at any point in time. So are we "in Christ."

Now that we have summarized what happened when we were born again, we will attempt to define the flesh. Our soul—mind, will, and emotions—was programmed by our old nature. Even though we now have a new nature and our souls have a new boss, the part of our mind, will, and emotions that is unrenewed to the leadership exchange wants life to go on as it always has. You can think of this as the ghost of the old man. This unrenewed part of our soul is the "flesh" or "self." That is why scripture tells us we are transformed into the image of Christ by the renewing of our mind. Only as the soul is renewed to thinking, choosing, and feeling, like our new boss, Jesus, will we appear to this world as vessels containing the life of Christ (Diagram 2.2).

Diagram 2.2

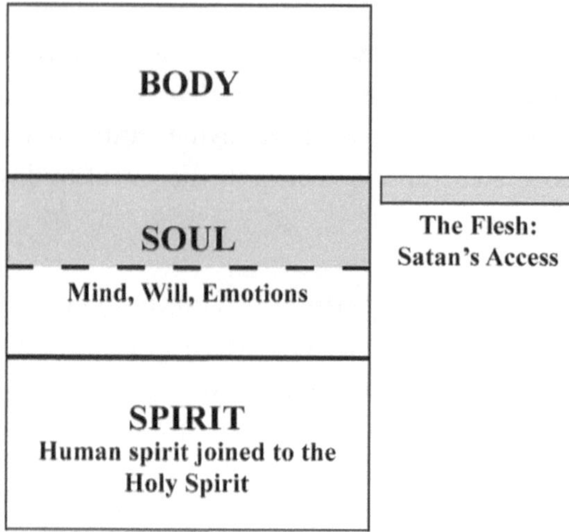

This is what you must remember. You have a soul, neutral in itself, but capable of great good or evil, depending on the force you *allow* to control it. Since we believe that as a Christian, your spirit cannot be inhabited by a demonic spirit, Satan's access to you is through your flesh. Consequently, whether from satanic attack or the influence of the flesh itself, both enter through the unrenewed part of the soul.

For this reason, from now on, we will not differentiate between the influence of the flesh or evil influence, with regard to a Christian. For a Christian, the bottom line is will you choose the power of the flesh or of the spirit, to control your soul (Diagram 2.3)? One leads to "corruption," and one leads to "eternal life" (Galatians 6:8).

Diagram 2.3

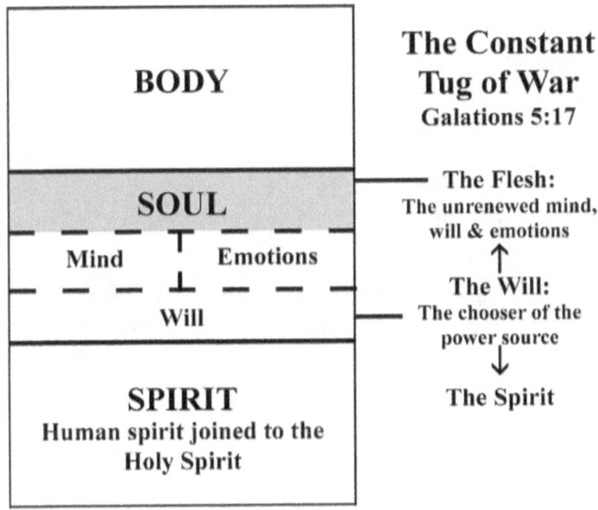

The choice is yours!

The last part of you as a person, which you need to understand, is your body. Remember, you are a spirit, encased in a soul, placed into a body. So your body, containing your soul, is the vessel holding the treasure of the life of Christ (Diagram 2.4).

In our discussion of your body, we will include all of the matter, including organs, which came from dust and will go back to dust. Even though you have probably not thought about it, when you die, your brain, which is a part of your earthly matter, will return to dust. It is your mind, as part of the soul, that lives on with your spirit.[2]

---

[2] The reason I am taking the stand that your soul will go on with your spirit, is that scripture teaches us we will know each other in eternity. Since the soul is the realm of the personality, which gives us our individuality as created beings, I believe the soul will go on into eternity with our spirit. Once we are delivered from the capacity to sin, there is nothing inherently evil in our soul.

Diagram 2.4

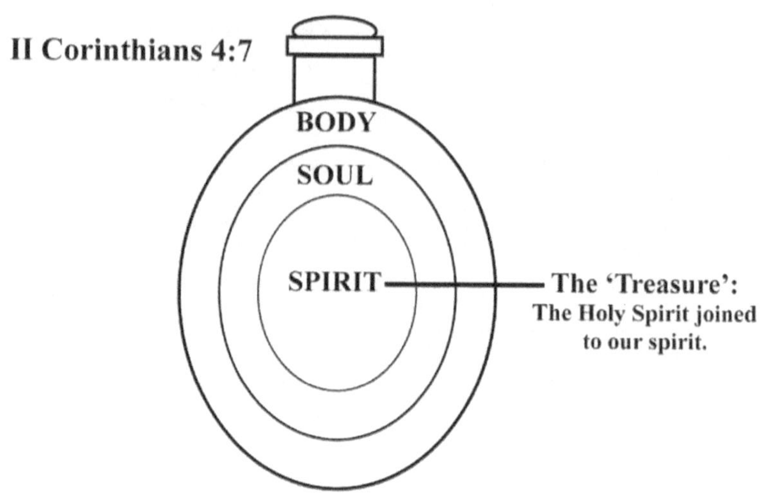

Since the brain is not the same as the mind, we need to understand the role they both play in our everyday lives. Our brain is actually the computer of our bodies. The mind is the computer operator. The operator can only process the information that is available in the computer. This is why it is so necessary to program our brains with the truth of God. The data we allow into our brains through our five senses is the information our minds will have to formulate. If the bulk of what we have programmed into our computers is godly, the mind will have godly data available to process. On the contrary, if we allow the thinking and morals of the world to freely enter our brains, our minds will have a harder time choosing righteousness.

What really controls our bodies, then, is our mind, rather than our brain. The signal the mind sends through the brain to direct the body is determined by the power source the will chooses. If our will chooses to yield to the flesh, then the mind will retrieve fleshly data from the brain and direct the body accordingly. Conversely, if our will chooses to follow the spirit, the mind will formulate godly data from the brain and direct the body in the ways of the Lord.

Which power source will you choose?

Diagram 2.5

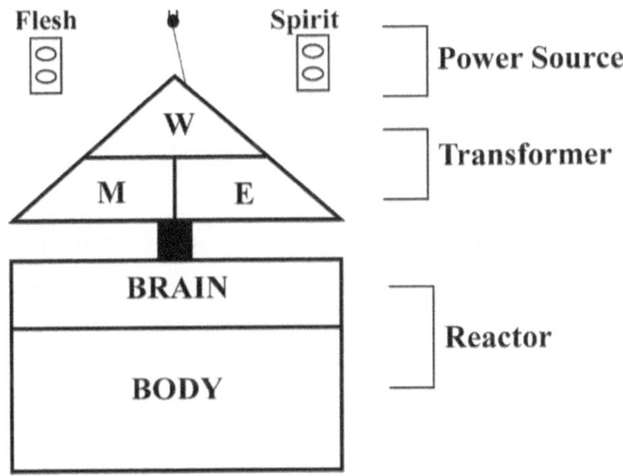

Therefore do not let sin reign in your mortal body
(Romans 6:12a)

Hopefully, you now have some understanding of your makeup as a human being and the war that rages within you. Even though Jesus took your "old man" with Him to the cross and consequently broke the power of sin in your life, unless your mind, will, and emotions are renewed, the flesh will remain strong; and it will be difficult for the spirit to win the tug of war portrayed in Diagram 2.3. When the spirit successfully convinces you to choose it as the power source, then the Spirit of God is allowed to flow through your soul, directing your body, and right deeds and attitudes come forth from the power of righteousness in the spirit man.

Personal Study

1. What are the power sources that fight for control of the soul in the unregenerate man? In a Christian?

    ____

    ____

    ____

2. Imagine the throne room in heaven as it is right now. Draw a simple diagram of God the Father, God the Son, and you, according to Ephesians 2:6 and Acts 2:33.

3. What is the definition of the flesh?
    What part does it play in hindering a walk of holiness?

    ____

    ____

    ____

4. What is a synonym for eternal life?

    ____

    ____

    ____

5. As a Christian, what is the function of your spirit, flesh, soul, and body?

    ____

    ____

    ____

6. What part of you includes your brain? What part of you includes your mind?

    ____

    ____

    ____

7. What part or parts of you will go to be with the Lord when your body dies?

    ____

    ____

    ____

CHAPTER 3

The Character of God

Now that we have looked at the makeup of man, we need to somewhat understand the character of the God that made him. Names had special meanings to God's people in the Old Testament. The names they chose for their children were representative of the circumstances surrounding the birth, what they felt toward the child, or what they wanted the child to be. So God, trying to give understanding of His infinite character to finite minds, gave His people different names for different attributes of Himself.

In Genesis chapter 1, God introduces Himself as "Elohim," which is written, capital "G," little "o," little "d," in the KJV, RSV, and NAS versions of the Bible. Anywhere you see "G," "o," "d," in the Old Testament, God is emphasizing the characteristics of Elohim. Elohim is a plural word introducing God in three persons: plurality, but yet one God.

Elohim also reveals the characteristic of a covenant God, the God who loves us so much He made covenant with Himself for our sake. God the Father, God the Son, and God the Holy Spirit made covenant with each other.

> For when God made the promise to Abraham, since He could swear by no one greater, He swore by Himself. (Hebrews 6:13)

When we see "God" in the Old Testament, we can think of the characteristic of Elohim, the covenant God, who loves us no matter what we do.

God introduces Himself to us first, as Elohim. When we first come to Jesus, we know Him as a God of unconditional love. We whine just a little, and He, in His understanding of our frailty, intervenes for us and changes our circumstances or reveals Himself to us in a special way. However, the time comes when God, in His unending love, endeavors to bring forth mature sons and daughters. He wants us to be like Him, just like any loving Father would.

In Genesis chapter 2, God introduces another name for Himself so that our finite minds can understand Him a little more. He yearns for fellowship with us. The more we understand His ways, the closer we will be to Him. In verse 4 of this chapter, we see God as capital "L," capital "O," capital "R," capital "D," "God." This notation of "LORD God" represents the name of God as Jehovah. God is showing Himself here as Jehovah Elohim. Why does He represent Himself now, as Jehovah? What is He now revealing about Himself?

Let's go back to our example of how we grow in our walk with the Lord. The day comes when suddenly we whine and God doesn't seem to hear. By the time we get to this point, we should understand God's ways enough to have some conception of faith and waiting on the Lord. We are now presented with a choice, we can choose to trust the Lord and believe He is working everything together for our good because He says He will, or we can choose to go by what we see around us and become discontent. The choice is ours. This is how God as Jehovah works in our lives. This is what Jehovah did in Genesis chapter 2.

God, as Jehovah, is looking for quality and righteousness. In order for righteousness to come forth in our lives, we must have a chance to choose unrighteousness. This is what God did in the garden. He chose the tree of the knowledge of good and evil and told Adam he would die the day he ate of it. We do not know if God ever intended for Adam to eat of the tree, but we do know it wasn't time in his growth for him to know the difference between good and evil. Jehovah gave Adam a choice because He desired that Adam, of his own free will, would choose righteousness. Of course, we know that Adam and Eve did not choose righteousness, and the resultant destruction. Jehovah knows the destruction of sowing to the flesh and in His love for us trains us to choose righteousness. The choice is always ours.

From Genesis chapters 1 and 2, we see God representing Himself as Elohim, Who loves us unconditionally no matter what we do and Who covenanted with Himself so our disobedience would not break the covenant. We also see God as Jehovah, who orchestrates the circumstances and trials in our lives to give us the opportunity to choose righteousness and become conformed to His image. Always remember, God loves you enough not to leave you as a "spoiled brat," but to train you up into Christlike character and maturity!

As we continue thinking about the character of God, we must understand that He is the source of any fruit of the Spirit. Flesh, including "good works," cannot produce real fruit. God is not just loving, He is love; not just faithful to us, His very nature is faithfulness; not just the giver of peace, He is peace; and on and on we could go. Why is this important to understand?

When you received Jesus as your Savior, you were born again, the old you passed away, and you became new.

> Therefore, if any man is in Christ, he is a new creature; the old things passed away; behold, new things have come. (II Corinthians 5:17)

II Peter 1:4 tells us we have become partakers of the divine nature. That word "partakers" means "having in common." The word "divine" means "that which proceeds from Himself." So we "have in common" "that which proceeds from Himself." We are now partakers of all the character or glory of God, because His nature now abides in us.

> When Christ, who is our life, is revealed, then you also will be revealed with Him in glory. (Colossians 3:4)

> Christ is our life and in Him…all the fullness of Deity
> dwells in bodily form. (Colossians 2:9)

What we must now understand is how God, Who wants us to be like Him, works to get what is supernaturally placed in us to show on the outside. Basically, there are two ways, desperation and death (to self, not our bodies). Physical death would transform us immediately. God wants us to be transformed by choosing righteousness. God tests us hoping we will choose righteousness and thus be transformed into His image. At the same time, we are unlikely to choose a path contrary to our will unless we have reached the point of desperation.

There is a survival instinct in our flesh that refuses to lie down and die. The stronger willed a person is, the more he will go through before he cries "uncle." God, in His desire for us to be like Him in this world (I John 4:17), allows Satan to arrange trials for us so we will fail to overcome them in our own strength. Satan thinks he is advancing his kingdom by harassing us and God is just looking at him pathetically, wondering when he is going to learn he is a defeated foe and cannot touch us apart from the lifting of God's hand. Always remember that what the enemy works for evil, God always works for our good (Genesis 50:20), to bring us to the glorious end He intends for us.

> For I know the plans that I have for you, declares the
> LORD, plans for welfare and not for calamity to give
> you a future and a hope. (Jeremiah 29:11)

God has a finished masterpiece in mind. Each one of us is a work of art that the *great designer* is completing.

> For I am confident of this very thing, that He who
> began a good work in you will perfect it until the day
> of Jesus Christ. (Philippians 1:6)

Not only is He completing the work, He is also the Creator of the work. He knows every flaw, inside and out. He knows what parts are of value and need to be brought out even more. He also loves His creation so much more than any other being. He is not content for the work to be so-so, but desires for it to be the masterpiece it was created to be.

The problem is this masterpiece cannot be made with human hands or with human strength. Only the Divine Life, which was birthed into the innermost parts of the creation, can do the work, and it can only do the work when the creation realizes the futility of any human effort and surrenders in total defeat to the Divine Life within. This is desperation!

When you finally come to the end of all self-effort, all will power; when you are worn out or totally disillusioned with "religion," then you are a candidate for the "power of His resurrection."

> That I may know Him, and the power of His resurrection and the fellowship of His suffering, being conformed to His death. (Philippians 3:10)

Until we get to the point of desperation, we will not choose the spirit to control our lives. This breaking process is painful, but it brings forth the "peaceful fruit of righteousness."

> All discipline for the moment seems not to be joyful, but sorrowful; yet to those who have been trained by it, afterwards it yields the peaceful fruit of righteousness. (Hebrews 12:11)

Keep your eyes on the Master and trust His love to allow only what is absolutely necessary to bring forth more glory in your life than you could have ever thought of. Enter every situation you would consider unpleasant with the excitement and anticipation of the good that God will bring forth from it; whether you ever see it with your eyes of flesh, or not, rest in it with eyes of faith.

When we finally come to the place of desperation, we are a candidate for death. Death must be chosen, and we will not let go of our "self-life" until we think there is a better option. Until we "hate even the garment spotted by the flesh" (Jude 23), we will not be willing to exchange our soiled garment for a righteous one.

Romans chapter 6 clearly tells us we are dead to sin. In other words, the part of us that desired to sin died with Jesus. Our new nature is Jesus who created us unto good works.

> For we are His workmanship, created in Christ Jesus
> for good works, which God prepared beforehand,
> that we should walk in them. (Ephesians 2:10)

If by faith in what God says in His word, I "consider myself dead unto sin, but alive unto God" (Romans 6:11), my mind, will, and emotions will be renewed; and I will think and feel like Jesus in that particular incident (because I have chosen to yield to His Spirit). The next time something happens where I am again faced with the choice of reacting like my flesh or like my spirit, I again must consider myself dead to sin and present the members of my body as instruments of righteousness to God, or I will walk after the flesh, which is just like I walked before I was born again, when my "old man" was alive.

> And do not go on presenting the members of your
> body to sin as instruments of unrighteousness; but
> present yourselves to God as those alive from the
> dead, and your members as instruments of righteous-
> ness to God. (Romans 6:13)

Every day of our lives, we will be presented with choices, by Jehovah. We can choose to walk after the flesh or after the spirit. The choice is ours.

We will get to the point where we will hate the flesh so much, and see so much flesh in ourselves, and so little of the righteousness within being worked out into our soul and body that we will again come to despair. It is at this point we must remember that human hands or strength cannot speed the work of the Master along any more than they could do the Master's work in the first place. We must rest in the Master's hands and know He will perfect that which concerns us.

> The LORD will perfect that which concerns me; Your mercy, O LORD, endures forever; Do not forsake the works of Your hands. (Psalm 138:8 (NKJV))

You can delay the divine work by not being surrendered and sensitive to His work in you, but you cannot rush the completion, for you are a masterpiece. You are the only one like you in the universe, living for all eternity, and the Divine Master is always on schedule.

Desperation and death are the tools the Lord uses to shape us into His own image, each of us individuals, but all with His character. By understanding the character of God, we can start to understand His working in our lives. By having an intimate relationship with Him, we can trust His love enough to abandon ourselves to the divine plan He has for us.

Personal Study

1. What characteristic of God does God's name of "Elohim" relate to us? How is it noted in the KJV, RSV, and NASV of the Bible?

2. What characteristic of God does God's name of "Jehovah" relate to us? How is it noted in the KJV, RSV, and NASV of the Bible?

3. Study Hebrews chapter 12:1–11, James 1:2–4, I Peter 1:6–7, I Peter 4:12–13, and Romans 5:3–4. Meditate on God's use of the trials in your life.

4. Read about the life of Joseph in Genesis 37:1 through Genesis 50:26. Think of what could have happened if Joseph had taken control of his life out of God's hands, at any particular time.

5. Study Romans chapter 6.

CHAPTER 4

A Scriptural Study of Desperation

But we have this treasure in earthen vessels, that the surpassing greatness of the power may be of God and not from ourselves; we are afflicted in every way, but not crushed; perplexed, but not despairing; persecuted, but not forsaken; struck down, but not destroyed; always carrying about in the body the dying of Jesus, that the life of Jesus also may be manifested in our body. For we who live are constantly being delivered over to death for Jesus' sake, that the life of Jesus also may be manifested in our mortal flesh. (II Corinthians 4:7–10)

We are vessels (Diagram 2:4) of the treasure that God has birthed within us. The treasure is more wonderful than anything we could ever imagine. Not only that, but when allowed, the treasure is so powerful that even the vessel starts to appear like the treasure. The effect is like radioactivity; it permeates and changes everything it touches. The problem is there was rotten flesh in the vessel before the treasure was deposited. Now, even though the rotten flesh is gone, there still is the leftover stench, referred to as the "flesh." The more the treasure is allowed to permeate the vessel, the more fragrant the vessel will seem and the less of the lingering smell will be noticed.

This truth is illustrated in the Old Testament story of Gideon. No matter how unworthy, how pathetic we think we are, the value is not in the vessel, but in the treasure. This is the necessity of desperation. As long as we think there is some worth in the vessel itself, or something worth salvaging from the old life, we will not depend totally on the treasure within us.

In Judges chapter 6, verse 15, Gideon answers God's request for him to deliver Israel with, "Oh Lord, how shall I deliver Israel? Behold my family is the least in Manasseh, and I am the youngest in my father's house." This could be a real understanding of the frailty of the flesh, of the total uselessness of self-effort, or it could be just an excuse. The point is this must be our conception of what we, left to ourselves, could do.

The Lord responds to Gideon the same way He responds to us. In verse 16 of chapter 6, He replies to Gideon, "surely I will be with you, and you shall defeat Midian as one man." In other words, "get your eyes off yourself; I know you can't win the battle! I don't need a warrior; I need someone who knows enough to know that without Me he can do nothing."

> I am the vine, you are the branches; he who abides in
> Me, and I in him, he bears much fruit; for apart from
> Me you can do nothing. (John 15:5)

This is exactly what God is saying to you and me. He is looking for willing vessels. He has all the power in the universe, and He has placed it in us. He is just waiting for us to come to the end of our own resources so He can be our source for everything and anything we do.

As we originally looked at in II Corinthians chapter 4, "we are afflicted in every way, but not crushed; struck down, but not destroyed" (verses 8,9). What is the purpose of this seemingly rough handling of the vessel? Unless we willful human vessels are placed into situations that we cannot handle in our own strength, we will not give up and depend on the treasure within (and believe me, some of us are strong willed enough to go to any extreme before we'll give up). So the work of our Heavenly Father continues, waiting for us to become so totally exhausted that we'll give up and rest in His arms.

An example of this is a swimmer who is drowning. Red Cross training teaches to allow the person to get exhausted before trying to save him. If an attempt is made to rescue him before exhaustion takes place, he will fight back and endanger the life of the one who is actually trying to save his life. We react in a similar way to God. Until we have become totally exhausted from our attempts to deliver ourselves—manipulate those around us, deny reality or any other flesh pattern we might have—we will not allow God to save us.

For the sake of our illustration, we will believe this is where Gideon was and that his reply to God was not an excuse for disobedience, or false humility. Our understanding of our bankruptcy in the flesh is absolutely necessary, but equally important is our unfailing confidence in the treasure within.

> I can do all things through Him who strengthens me.
> (Philippians 4:13)

This is not a strengthening of the self-life, but an infusion of strength in the inner man, such as fiberglass threads through a plastic tarp. Of ourselves, we can do nothing, but if the life of Christ within us is allowed to use our souls and bodies, there is nothing that cannot be done.[3]

Another aspect of the story of Gideon that must be understood is found in chapter 7 of Judges. In verse 2, the Lord says to Gideon:

> The people who are with you are too many for Me
> to give Midian into their hands, lest Israel become
> boastful, saying, 'My own power has delivered me.'

---

[3] In many instances, Philippians 4:13 is used inappropriately as a magic formula to enable us to overextend ourselves, do things, and go in directions that God never intended for us. God provides when and where He leads—not necessarily where our flesh, or others, want us to go.

God will not share His glory! Not only that, but if there is anyway our flesh can claim to have had something to do with a victory, we will take part of the glory for ourselves. As long as we have not reached the point of desperation, we will keep trying and will not choose death to our self-life and yield control of our life to Christ. God, in His loving wisdom, arranges our trials—through the lifting of His force field of love around us—so every avenue of escape from total dependence on Him is cut off. Once we finally quit fighting the Spirit for control of our lives, the victory is already won.

> But thanks be to God, who gives us the victory
> through our Lord Jesus Christ. (I Corinthians 15:57)

The Lord continues through verse 7 of chapter 7 of Judges to thin down Gideon's army so there is no way he could have victory in the natural. When we finally give up on the natural, we are candidates for the supernatural, but it is amazing how long it takes us to realize this!

> For whoever wishes to save his life (self-life) shall lose
> it; but whoever loses his life (self-life) for My sake
> shall find it (Christ's life). (Matthew 16:25 (emphasis
> mine))

Now the Lord has the circumstances just the way He wants them and tells Gideon how the victory will come. In verse 16 of chapter 7, Gideon's divinely directed plan gives us a picture of what we have available. We must remember Christ had not yet come to earth as a man and had not yet been resurrected; so Gideon did not have divine life within Him. Gideon tells his men to take a torch in one hand and to place an earthen pitcher over the flame. In the other hand, they are to have a trumpet. The torch, being light, represents *the Light of the world*" (John 9:5), who is Jesus. The only thing stopping the light from shining is the earthen vessel, the pitcher. Jesus, the light, lives in every born-again person. The only thing stopping His light from penetrating the darkness of this world is the earthen vessel made up of our body and souls. As we see in verse 20 of chapter 7, the light of the torches is revealed when the pitchers are broken. So it is with us. Brokenness is represented by an attitude of complete dependence on the life within us. Desperation is the doorway to brokenness.

As the story comes to an end, we see what happens when, in total obedience and dependence on the Lord, the pitchers are broken and the light is revealed—total victory, given by God, without any fighting on the part of Gideon and his men. When the all-powerful, divine life within us is allowed to shine through broken vessels, God fights for us, and we just collect the spoil. It sounds so easy; why is it rarely realized?

Few Christians ever get to the place of brokenness and total dependence on God. In any given instance, our flesh is in control, or the Spirit of God is in control. There is no in-between. Unless, in utter dependence on God, we consciously yield control of each situation to the Spirit, our flesh will be in control, and we will not see Gideon's victory. Eventually, you will automatically be so aware that it is Christ who lives in you and not the old you; you won't have to continually think about yielding. You will get to the point where you would dread the thought of the old you being in control of your life. However, in the beginning of this walk, you will have to work at renewing your mind, will, and emotions.

Let's review what we have just learned with Gideon. When we are born again, God exchanges our old nature for His divine nature, and Jesus becomes our new life. We don't necessarily feel any different than we did before we were born again and do not necessarily act or think differently, because the change happened in our spirit, not in our soul or body. Some old habits, addictions, thoughts, negative feelings, and other remnants of the old nature drop off immediately when we are born again, but many do not. In other words, we have a lit torch and an unbroken pitcher.

Gradually, God gently allows trials and circumstances in our lives to break the pitcher so the light can shine out. As the light shines forth, it also gradually purifies the pitcher. The light so permeates the pitcher, it is much more beautiful broken than it was whole—we have become vessels of honor.

> Therefore, if a man cleanses himself from these things,
> he will be a vessel for honor, sanctified, useful to the
> Master, prepared for every good work. (II Timothy 2:21)

Now, going back to II Corinthians chapter 4, let's look at the description of the breaking process given here. We already referred to verses 8 and 9 with their description of the trials of life; now let's look at verse 10: "Always carrying about in the body the dying of Jesus, that the life of Jesus also may be manifested in our body." This speaks of absolute surrender, even unto death. Many of us wouldn't mind dying for Jesus so we could leave this world, but being a living sacrifice and giving thanks to Him for everything He allows in our life is another matter.

> I urge you therefore, brethren, by the mercies of God,
> to present your bodies a living and holy sacrifice,
> acceptable to God, which is your spiritual service and
> worship. (Romans 12:1)

> In everything give thanks; for this is God's will for
> you in Christ Jesus. (I Thessalonians 5:18)

The promised result of our walking this life as if we are dead is Jesus being seen in our body, or in other words, in our performance. If we will be living sacrifices, surrendered unto any use in life, or unto death, then the pitcher will finally be broken and the light will be released. Remember, when the light is released, God supernaturally arranges the victory without us fighting the war. This is the good news of the gospel!

Today, I challenge you to reach the point of desperation. Will you get so sick and tired of running your life that you will give God control, no matter what He allows? Don't listen to your flesh as it screams out all the things that will happen if you give up control. God loves you more than you will ever know. He will not allow any more pressure than is necessary, and He promises no more than you can bear, that is, with His grace. Your flesh must have more than it can bear or you won't give up control. His yoke is easy and His burden is light, but that means His *yoke* must be in place. Give up, ask for His yoke, and enter into His rest.

> Come to Me, all who are weary and heavy-laden, and I will give you rest. Take My yoke upon you, and learn from Me, for I am gentle and humble in heart; and you shall find rest for your souls. (Matthew 12:28–29)

> There remains therefore a Sabbath rest for the people of God. For the one who has entered His rest has himself also rested from his works, as God did from His. Let us therefore be diligent to enter that rest, lest anyone fall through following the same example of disobedience. (Hebrews 4:9–11)

Personal Study

1. Study the story of Gideon in Judges chapter 6, verse 11 through chapter 7, verse 25. Meditate on the correlation between this account of Gideon's life and your life.

2. Write out Isaiah 30:15.

3. Think of ways in your own life that you can now see God "thinning down your army" so that you will give Him all the glory. It is an exciting place to be when there is no human way out because if we wait on Him and don't make a way of escape, we will see God move mountains.

4. Look up at least five references from a concordance, as to Jesus being light. Meditate on these.

5. Look up at least five references in a concordance, on you being a vessel. Meditate on these.

Chapter 5

A Scriptural Study of Death

Or do you not know that all of us who have been baptized into Christ Jesus have been baptized into His death? Therefore we have been buried with Him through baptism into death, in order that as Christ was raised from the dead through the glory of the Father, so we too might walk in newness of life. For if we have become united with Him in the likeness of His death, certainly we shall be also in the likeness of His resurrection, knowing this, that our old self was crucified with Him, that our body of sin might be done away with, that we should no longer be slaves to sin; for he who has died is freed from sin. (Romans 6:3–7)

Although the thought of studying the subject of death probably has never seemed exciting, we must remember that after death comes resurrection life with all its benefits. Jesus Himself, once He entered this world as a man, had to die before He could once again be glorified. Death precedes resurrection life.

Unless a grain of wheat falls into the earth and dies, it remains by itself alone; but if it dies it bears much fruit. He who loves his life loses it; and he who hates his life in this world shall keep it to–life eternal. (John 12:24–25)

If you aren't dissatisfied with the life (bios)[4] you have, you will not be willing to die for real life (zoe)[5]. The slang phrase, "Get a life!" is much more real than the world will ever know.

In the case of a Christian, real life (zoe) is present at new birth, but the experience of zoe life will not be realized until the experience of death is allowed to be worked in our lives. In order for us to allow the experience of death to affect our lives, we must have a revelation of the need for dying, or we will shrink back from the pain. We must know with a certainty that the only way out of this life (bios) into His life (zoe) is death. Without this renewing of the mind, we will take any other avenue but death. Death is always a last resort.

Let's consider the Romans chapter 6 account of what happened when we were born again. As we have pointed out in previous chapters, when we received Christ as our Savior, we received His life. We were baptized into Christ. We are now "in Him," and He is in us. There are no boundaries or distance in the spirit. When the Spirit of God made our spirit alive, He joined our spirit. Remember the analogy used in chapter 2. If we pour a bottle of cola into a glass, and then pour a bottle of orange soda into the same glass, we no longer have orange or cola, just a glass of soda. They are both present in the glass, but no longer separable. So it is with our spirit man. Our spirit is blended with the Spirit of Christ—we are united with Him. The question is what did getting baptized into Christ do for us?

Since we were immersed into the life of Christ when we were born again, we became united with a River of Life with no beginning or end. So, when Jesus died, we died. That is, our old self died with Him. When Jesus was buried, we were buried with Him. When He defeated the forces of hell, we were "in Him," and when He rose from the grave, so did we. Romans chapter 6 tells us we were raised to *"newness of life."* That means we got a new life (zoe), and we left our old life in the grave. After Jesus was resurrected, He went to sit at the right hand of the Father, and so did we (Ephesians 2:6).

____

4   see Appendix II

5   ibid

If we will choose to identify with the death that Christ experienced, then we will also experience the glory of resurrection life (Romans 6:5). We will experience the same life (zoe) that Jesus has. Jesus can become our life in experience, not just as a matter of fact. The only way we can get rid of our old life is through identifying with Christ's crucifixion. Our old man was crucified with Christ when we were born again, but to experience the reality of this, we must consider it to be true, no matter what our flesh tries to tell us. That is why Roman 6:11 tells us to "consider yourselves to be dead to sin, but alive to God in Christ Jesus." This obviously is a walk of faith, because we know our flesh is still alive and well! This walk of faith is further expressed in Galatians 2:20:

> I have been crucified with Christ; and it is no longer
> I who live, but Christ lives in me; and the life which I
> now live in the flesh I live by faith in the Son of God,
> who loved me, and delivered Himself up for me.

In other words, by faith in what the Bible says, we are dead, even though we can still be seen and heard. Then what is dead and what is alive? Our old man or old nature (synonymous terms) is dead. It was crucified with Christ. So we are dead. Remember, who you really are is a spirit, who has a soul, who lives in a body. The part of you that has life (bios) isn't important. It is just the vessel that carries the treasure. Our old nature is now replaced with the nature of Jesus. So Jesus is now our life, and we consider this to be true by faith because the exchange was not something we could see or feel.

The longer we walk, knowing it is not the old man inside our body anymore, but Jesus; the more our mind, will, and emotions will be renewed. When our mind, will, and emotions start to think, choose, and feel like our new nature, who is Jesus, we will have the mind of Christ and display the fruit of the Spirit. This is not merely hypothetical—this is reality!

For the most part, the body of Christ does not understand the whole gospel. We are taught how to get to heaven, but not that heaven is in us. The term the "Kingdom of Heaven" or the "Kingdom of

God" in scripture does not speak of just an eternal home. Jesus said, "the kingdom of God is at hand" (Matthew 4:17). In other words, it is here and now. The definition of the "Kingdom of God" in the *Vine's Expository Dictionary* is: "The sovereign rule of God, manifested in Christ, to defeat His enemies, with a people over whom He reigns, and a realm in which the power of His reign is experienced."

We entered the Kingdom of Heaven when we were born again. We will experience the Kingdom of Heaven, as, by faith, we consider this true and, by surrender, allow the King to rule. We were taught correctly that we had to die to enter the Kingdom of Heaven, but might not have understood what part had to die—and when. A portion of scripture that clearly shows our entering the Kingdom of Heaven upon new birth is Colossians 1:13–14.

> For He delivered us from the domain of darkness, and
> transferred us to the kingdom of His beloved Son, in
> whom we have redemption, the forgiveness of sins.

We were transferred, transplanted, or delivered from where the god of this world rules, into the realm where Jesus rules (Diagram 5:1). Since Jesus is God, we can refer to His realm as the Kingdom of God. *Delivered* is in past tense, so we know it is something that has already happened. The remaining question then is when were we delivered?

Diagram 5:1

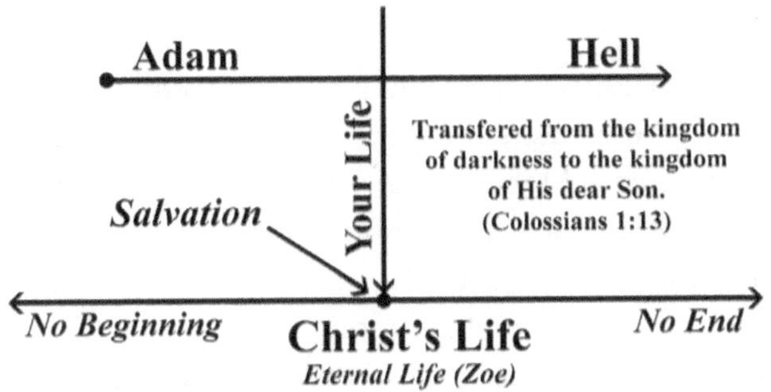

If we go up one verse from Colossians 1:13 to verse 12, we see that we were "qualified to share in the inheritance of the saints" when we were delivered from the domain of darkness. Thus, we received our inheritance as saints and were transferred to the Kingdom of Heaven at the same time—when we were born again. If we were delivered out of one realm, we automatically have to be somewhere else. So when we received Christ as our Savior, we were plucked out of the crowd going along the broad highway to hell and were safely placed into the Kingdom of God.

> The Lord is my shepherd, I *shall* not want. He *makes* me lie down in green pastures; He *leads* me beside quiet waters. He *restores* my soul; He *guides* me in the paths of righteousness For His name's sake. (Psalm 23:1–4)

All of the verbs in italics in Psalm 23 are in the present tense. Even our use of Psalm 23 as the great funeral text is a bit at liberty. In the spirit, which is reality, we are lying in lush green grass, next to the most peaceful water you have ever imagined, with no care or worry. This is the Kingdom of God, and we are already citizens of it!

> If then you have been raised up with Christ, keep seeking the things above, where Christ is, seated at the right hand of God. Set your mind on the things above, not on the things that are on earth. For you have died and your life is hidden with Christ in God. (Colossians 3:1–3)

We have to know what our benefits as children of God are, or we will never use them. Imagine that your biological father is a wealthy businessman. He is influential and has a gorgeous estate with lush gardens, a huge swimming pool with hot tub, and sauna, and money is absolutely no object. The problem is your mother left your father when you were a baby and remarried a simple hill dweller. She never told you who you really are. You are the child of the businessman. and you think you are the child of the simple hill dweller. You are as influential as a grasshopper, you live in a shack and swim in the creek, and poor isn't even an accurate description of your financial status. What's wrong? You don't know who you are!

Until we have such a strong understanding of who we really are that it gets from our head to our heart, we will not experience the benefits of who we are in the spirit. Consequently, we will still let the enemy—in partnership with our flesh—rule, torment, and condemn us and kill, steal, and destroy as if he has the authority to do so when, in reality, we are no longer in his domain. What a waste of what Jesus has done for us that would be!

Ask the Lord to open up the eyes of your understanding, "that you may know the riches of the glory of His inheritance in the saints" (Ephesians 1:18). Don't settle for anything less, not one bit less than what is yours in Christ Jesus. Your Heavenly Father loves you so much that He paid a very great price that this inheritance might be yours. Don't waste what He purchased for you with the death of His only Son.

Personal Study

1. What is the difference between bios and zoe life? Study Appendix II until you fully comprehend the difference.

2. Look up the word "immersed" in a Bible dictionary. Meditate on what this reveals about your spiritual condition.

3. Look up the word "nature" in a Bible dictionary. Meditate on how a new nature should affect you.

4. Look up at least five references to the Kingdom of God or the Kingdom of Heaven, in a Bible concordance. Concentrate on how the correct understanding of these phrases could possibly change your interpretation of these five scriptures.

5. Meditate on I Peter 4:1–2.[6]

---

[6] Note: The NASB states, *"Christ has suffered in the flesh"* and *"he who has suffered in the flesh has ceased from sin."* The footnote in the NAS Harper Study Bible actually states, *"Christ has suffered death in the flesh"* and the context would allow the second portion to also read, *"he who has suffered death in the flesh has ceased from sin."*

CHAPTER 6

Putting on the New When You Feel Like the Old

By this point in our study of The Exchanged Life. you should understand the old you no longer lives but Christ lives in you. By faith, we consider what the Bible says about our death, burial, and resurrection with Christ to be true. We then have to come to the place of desperation, or the end of our own self-effort, before we give up trying to live like Christ and let Him live through us. Knowing all this then, how do we stop acting like the old man and start acting like the new?

First of all, know the exchanging of the old ways for the new ways is a very gradual process. Usually, the change is so gradual we hardly see it in ourselves and someone else has to recognize it for us. Don't become discouraged when you feel like you are not getting anywhere. The biggest temptation you will face is losing your faith in the biblical truths regarding the exchanged life and giving up. When I was at the point of despairing that I would never change in one particular area of my life, the Lord spoke to my heart that He was the One who would "perfect that which concerns me" and His "mercy… endures forever" (Psalm 138:8 NKJV). In other words, no matter how long it takes to change us into His image, He will never become impatient, tired, or give up on us as hopeless. God has eternity to work on us. We must rest in His restoration schedule.

I cannot overemphasize the pitfall of discouragement. To walk by faith means we will not see or feel what the Bible says is true. Eventually, faith becomes sight, but in the beginning, it is all by faith. That means, even if my emotions feel like I hate someone, I know that Jesus loves them. Now, I also know that Jesus is my new nature and the nature of someone or something determines what it acts like. If I react according to my nature (who I really am), I can choose to love the person my emotions feel hatred toward.

Now don't get frantic. You cannot change an emotion. It is God's grace that changes us. Scripture tells us what God's best is for us, but without the power of grace, the Bible could become a hard task master's list of things to do. This would lead to a heavy yoke of bondage, discouragement, and a rejection of the Christian life as something too hard to bear.

As soon as you recognize an unbiblical emotion, also recognize where it is coming from. Your old nature was crucified with Christ, so it's not coming from your old nature (Diagram 2.2). In our illustration, the emotion of hate is coming from the flesh. We are actually dead to the unbiblical emotion of hate because the part of us that could hate—our old nature—is dead. Our new nature, who is Jesus, does not hate. If we act according to who we really are, we will not hate either. We are dead to sin (Romans 6:7). The only time we will sin is when we yield to the flesh rather than to the spirit (Diagram 2.3). If our flesh is empowering our soul, we will produce dead works at best, evil at the worst, both being sin and "the wages of sin is death" (Romans 6:23). "For the one who sows to his own flesh will from the flesh reap corruption" (Galatians 6:8a). If your spirit, which is united with the Holy Spirit, is empowering your soul, you will produce the fruit of the Spirit. "The one who sows to the Spirit shall from the Spirit reap eternal life" (Galatians 6:8b). Remember, eternal life is synonymous with Christ's life.

The problem is you still feel like you hate the person. This is the crucial point in winning the battle between the flesh and the spirit. You must consider yourself dead to hatred (Romans 6:11) even when your emotions are raging. If, by faith, you take this stand, no matter how many times or how often your flesh flares up, eventually your flesh will give in, and you will feel love. At this point, that portion of your flesh has been renewed. Every time the spirit wins a battle, the flesh loses a little more power (think of less shaded area in Diagram 2.2). The spirit will win the tug of war a little easier the next time because there is less weight on the flesh's team (Diagram 2.3). Remember, the change is so minute it may not be noticeable for months or even years. If you don't faint in the tug of war, you are guaranteed the victory!

> But thanks be to God, who gives us the victory
> through our Lord Jesus Christ. (I Corinthians 15:57)

This is the fight of faith! The enemy's temptation will always be to get us to believe in what we can see, hear, or feel, rather than to believe, by faith, what God has said to be true. If Satan can get us to believe a lie, then he has us where he wants us. We must remember that truth is what God's word says about a situation. The word of the Lord may come directly to our hearts through the Holy Spirit or from another believer in the form of prophecy, a word of knowledge, or a word of wisdom. God may also speak through the divinely illumined words of a speaker or directly from the written word. Regardless of how God's word comes, it is the unveiling of God's perfect will, and Satan will always try to snatch the word from our heart. Stand on the word of God, against all that is contrary to it, and He will bring it to pass.

As stated previously, the unrenewed part of our mind, will, and emotions that was programmed by our old nature makes up our flesh. Our flesh makes us painfully aware we are very much human. Only by thoroughly renewing our minds to the truth of who we are in Christ will we be able to consistently win the war against the flesh in the face of our humanity. We are new creations, and we have a new nature. If we believe this is true, our new nature should determine how we act.

Why then does it seem so difficult to "put on the new self" (Colossians 3:10)? The problem is we go by what our flesh is thinking or feeling rather than standing on the truth that our old nature is dead and we have a new nature who is Christ Jesus.

This is the crucial point. If we do not believe the truth about who we are in Christ, we will believe the lies of the flesh, and we will not be victorious. We must react to our flesh like a gorilla behind bars. It can shake the bars, growl, jump up and down, and carry on all it wants to, but it's on one side of the bars and we are on the other. Our flesh can have perverted thoughts, rant and rave, be down and depressed, or be an anxious mess, but all of these symptoms are just the "ghost of the old man," and he's on one side of the grave and we are on the other (Diagram 6.1). Will you believe it?

Diagram 6.1

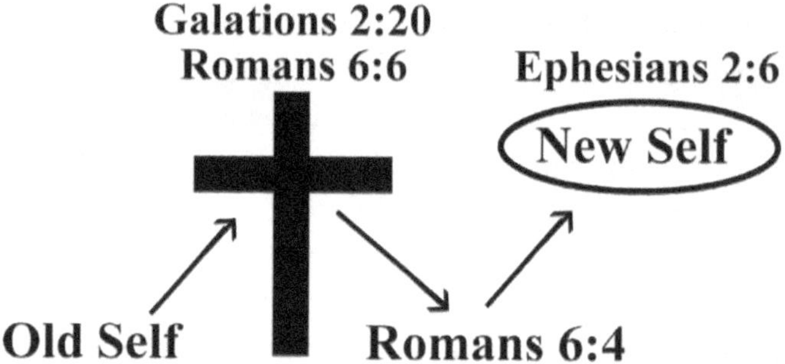

Therefore consider the members of your earthly body as dead to immorality, impurity, passion, evil desire, and greed, which amounts to idolatry. For it is on account of these things that the wrath of God will come and in them you also once walked, when you were living in them. But now you also, put them aside: anger, wrath, malice, slander and abusive speech from your mouth. Do not lie to one another, since you laid aside the old self with its evil practice, and have put on the new self who is being renewed to a true knowl-

edge according to the image of the One who created
him. (Colossians 3:5–10)

As we look at Colossians 3:5–10, we see verse 5 is telling us to consider the members of our body as dead to immorality. How can we be dead to sin when we know we still commit sinful acts? Who we really are is spirit, which is the seat of our nature. We are partakers of the divine nature, which is the nature of Jesus. Jesus did not and does not sin. Neither can we sin, in our spirit, which is who we really are. The problem lies in whether we choose to let the flesh or whether we choose to let the spirit empower our soul. This is how we put on the new self. The new self is our new nature, which is in our spirit. When we choose to yield to the spirit, we *put on the new self.* The part of us that had no choice but to sin is dead, that is, our old nature. So who we really are, which is our spirit, is alive to God but dead to sin.

It is like looking in the closet to decide what to wear. There are two outfits that can be worn. One outfit is the flesh, which is the shadow of our old nature, and the other outfit is the spirit, which represents the nature of God. Which one will you choose to put on? The one you choose will determine what you will look like to those around you, just as a change of clothes would.

In verse 7 of Colossians chapter 3, we see the literalness of the exchanged life. We once walked like the list in verse 5 of chapter 3. Our very existence was a life characterized by sin. Maybe not this exact list, but sin nonetheless. We once walked that way because that was our nature, but now we are not expected to live like that because we have a new life to live out of. Those things we are to put off are shadows from our old life, because we are not the same person anymore. We have a new life and are new creations. We are literally no longer "living in them" (Colossians 3:7). Not because of the change in our outward behavior, but because of the change in our nature. Change comes from the inside out. Our changing of the outward, through willpower, will never change the inward. This is the truth of the gospel. The inward was changed when we were born again so there would be a power source to change the outward. We are new creations! The new life within us can make us holy like He is holy, but we must know the truth and choose to walk according to the truth we now know.

When we choose to walk according to the truth, the truth will set us free from our old selves and renew us into the image of the One who created us. The truth will gradually change our outward performance, until our behavior lines up with who we are inside. Then we will begin to appear new to those around us, and they will call us Christians, because we really do act like our Savior. We continually put on (believe we are) the new self, even when we still feel very much like the old. As our "feelers" get renewed, we will even start to "feel" brand new!

Personal Study

1. Write down five ways in which you think, feel, or act differently now than you did before you were born again. Meditate on how much the Lord has already changed you maybe more than you realize.

    ____

    ____

    ____

2. How would you expect a creature with the nature of Jesus to act? Since you are that creature, by faith, expect yourself to be changed into Christ's image (already new on the inside and gradually being changed on the outside).

    ____

    ____

    ____

3. Write out two verses, besides Psalm 138:8, that assure us the work of changing us into the image of Christ is God's job, not ours.

    ____

    ____

    ____

CHAPTER 7

Unconditional Surrender

There is a way which seems right to a man and the
end thereof are the ways of death. (Proverbs 14:12)

Whose way are you following?

It is great to know that the character of God is to work all things together for our good. All the knowledge and power of the God that created the universe is on our side. It is mind boggling to know we are crucified with Christ and have received a new nature, the very nature of God Himself. It is also awesome to know we were in Christ when He defeated the powers of darkness and made public show of them. Nonetheless, with all this being true, the tragic truth is we can live totally defeated lives if we remain in control of our lives instead of Christ.

The Christian life can be compared to a wheel with a hub at the center. The only way the wheel can run in balance is with Jesus in the center as the hub of our lives. The spokes of the wheel represent our family and friends, cares and concerns, and responsibilities and activities. The spokes are all connected to the center, but unless each one stems from an intimate relationship with Jesus, our lives will not run smoothly. Furthermore, if we allow any one of the spokes to crowd out Jesus as the center, our lives will be off-balance, becoming increasingly lopsided and of less use in the Kingdom of God.

Regretfully, the majority of truly born-again believers fall into the lopsided category. They have received Christ as Savior and are at various degrees of maturity but have someone or something—other than Jesus—at the center of their lives. This lopsided condition is not exclusive to young believers but can exist at any stage of Christian growth.

The Israelites' escape from Egypt is also a picture of the Christian life. Egypt represents the world. When we were born again, God "delivered us from the domain of darkness, and transferred us to the kingdom of His beloved Son" (Colossians 1:13). This means we were set free from the power of this world's system. This is symbolized by the nation of Israel's deliverance out of Egypt, through the Red Sea, to the wilderness. It was only a few days' journey to the Promised Land, but due to doubt and unbelief, they failed to enter the land. Instead, they wandered around in the wilderness for the remainder of their lives with the exception of Joshua and Caleb, who believed the word of the Lord. The Jews in the wilderness were like many people today—born again, but off-balance—having someone or something in the center of their lives other than Jesus. Just as the Israelites aimlessly spent their lives in the wilderness, if we remain off-balance, we too can miss what God has for our lives.

Being off-balance also puts undue wear on the rubber of our wheels. Our bodies and souls were designed to run with Jesus as the center of our lives. When He is not the center, we develop adverse symptoms in our soul and bodies. If you are suffering from anxiety, depression, mental illness, paranoia, or any other disorder of your mind or emotions, your symptoms are indicating Jesus is not in control of your life. Eventually, the symptoms in your soul may affect your body, causing psychosomatic illness. The root of all of this is an out-of-balance life, resulting in unnecessary wear on your body and soul. Only by surrendering to the Lord's control of your life and revolving your life around Him (not around service for Him) can these symptoms start to be reversed.

Let me tell you the story of when I entered into the reality of the exchanged life. The counselor I was referred to for treatment of my extreme anxiety and depression looked me right in the eye and told me my problem wasn't my circumstances, but my problem was I was in control of my life. I could not believe what I was hearing.

I thought I was totally committed to the Lord; my life overflowed with good works. I was a victim of tragic circumstance and he had the audacity to tell me my problem was I was in control of my life. What nerve! But he was absolutely right. It took him a good part of an hour to wade through my well-meaning self-righteousness before he could even begin to shake my confidence in my belief that Jesus was already in control of my life. You see I had placed Jesus on the throne of my heart every time the teaching was presented to me. I never missed an altar call for total surrender, and I really believed I had given the Lord control of my life. What finally convinced me? The counselor explained that when Jesus is in control of our lives, He is also in control of our mind, will, and emotions. When the Spirit of Christ within us is in control of our emotions, then we will feel and react like Jesus. The fruit of the Spirit (Galatians 5:22) is the list of what Jesus being in control is like. When He is in control, there will be peace instead of anxiety, joy instead of depression, trust instead of fear, and hope in the place of despair.

If you are wondering how a person gets to the place of unconditional surrender, when someone as zealous as me was not there, that is a good question. You see, zeal has nothing to do with surrender. For that matter, knowledge and years of walking with the Lord have nothing to do with surrender. Surrender is similar in nature to repentance. Repentance is a change of mind, a change in the way we think. Remember, "there is a way which seems right to a man" (Proverbs 14:12), and that is not God's way. Repentance is getting sick and tired enough of the status quo that we want change no matter what it costs us. If it costs us getting out of the director's chair and letting Jesus take over, we are willing to do it.

What would have to happen in your life before you would look forward to a change in chief executive officer? Until you see the way which *seems right* to you ends in death, you will not be willing to give up control. Death in this usage is the outcome of anything done in the power of the flesh, which includes your own strength. The Bible describes such an approach to life as a *ministry of death.*

> Not that we are adequate in ourselves to consider any-
> thing as coming from ourselves, but our adequacy is
> from God, who also made us adequate as servants of a
> new covenant, not of the letter, but of the Spirit, for the
> letter kills, but the Spirit gives life. But if the *ministry
> of death*, in letters engraved on stones, came with glory,
> so that the sons of Israel could not look intensely at the
> face of Moses because of the glory of his face, fading
> as it was, how shall the ministry of the Spirit fail to be
> even more with glory? (II Corinthians 3:5–8)

It is not until we really see the futility of our own way that we are willing to go through the fight our flesh will give us when we give up control. Our old man ruled our lives before we were born again, and the flesh still wants to rule just like the old man. Again, the old nature's power is broken, but the flesh will only take its place of defeat when the power of the cross is continually applied to it. My vivid imagination pictures this like the use of a cross for protection in a vampire movie. Until the flesh knows you know who is boss, it will continue to fight for control in every area of your life.

When in desperation, you surrender to Christ's unconditional control of your life; the flesh will have to take its place of defeat, in the face of resurrection power. Christ's life, which is now your life, will replace flesh as the power source (Diagram 2:5), and Christ's rule produces abundant life rather than death.

In order for us to want a change in our lives more than any-thing, we must be honest with ourselves and see our lives as they really are. Before my appropriation of the exchanged life, I used to try and convince myself that what I was experiencing in my Christian walk was as good as it could get on earth. I knew my Bible well, so I knew I was supposed to be having abundant life. Consequently, I assumed that what I was experiencing was as good a life on this earth as you could have. Even though I struggled with anxiety, I assumed I must have had the peace that surpasses understanding, because after years of doing all the "right things," my peace level wasn't getting any higher. Although I was plagued with bouts of depression, I figured

I had fullness of joy because of my faithfulness to the Lord and my religious activity.

The only thing that finally changed my mind was my physical reaction to the circumstances God had so carefully allowed, to bring me to the end of my own self-effort. My dedication in striving to live a "perfect" Christian life had become my own worst enemy. If I had cared less about the things of God, I would have had no trouble in admitting I was going the wrong way, but my experience was more like the Apostle Paul's life before the Damascus Road, "concerning the law I was without blame" (Philippians 3:6).

What then, finally convinced me? My circumstances had left me in such a state of despair my hands literally shook. I cried out to God all day to take my life so the agony would end and took prescription drugs at night so I could block out reality. That day in the counseling office, I was told my hands would not be shaking from anxiety if Christ were in control of my life. I was finally convinced I could not go on in the condition I was in and that I had nothing to lose by identifying with Christ's death, burial, and resurrection. That day, I decided my way was definitely leading to death, so maybe I really was in control of my life. The "old me" took my place of death with Jesus and was buried with Jesus. and when He arose, I arose with a new life—His life. A most remarkable thing took place during that counseling session. The "old me" had died, and the "new me," with Jesus in control, did not shake for when Christ is in control of our lives, it is His life that is seen in us and Jesus is not anxious.

This brings us to a very important point. How do we know when we are in control of our lives? When we are in control, the fruit of the Spirit will not be present. We may try to convince ourselves, as I did, that it does not get any better, but if we are honest with ourselves, we will know that we hunger and thirst for more.

If we live with anxiety, depression, doubt, fear, or any other way contrary to abundant life, Jesus is not in control of our life at that moment in time. Even after our knowledge of our co-crucifixion with Christ, and our initial surrender to Him, self (synonymous with flesh) will continually try to rule our lives. This is the battle spoken of in Romans chapter 7 (Diagram 2.3).

> For that which I am doing, I do not understand, for I am not practicing what I would like to do, but I am doing that very thing I hate. But if I do the very thing I do not wish to do, I agree with the Law; confessing that it is good. So now, no longer am I the one doing it, but sin which indwells me. For I know that nothing good dwells in me, that is, in my flesh; for the wishing is present in me, but the doing of the good is not. For the good that I wish, I do not do; But I practice the very evil that I do not wish. (Romans 7:15–25)

Romans chapter 7 speaks of the defeat in our lives when Jesus is not in control. Although we may be capable of producing good works on our own, operating from self-effort is of the flesh, no matter how good our works look. We must remember that either the flesh is in control or the Spirit of Christ is in control—there is no middle ground.

The mind-set of having to perform in certain ways to be approved of God is also misleading. This is actually a definition of the law referred to in Romans chapter 7. The law was a list of what you needed to do to be blessed by God and the curses that would result if you didn't. Our flesh wants to think it can do something to gain God's approval so we can always recognize our flesh, when we feel accepted or not accepted by God according to our good or bad performance. The gospel says we are accepted by God because of Jesus' performance. What a contrast!

This brings us back to the Apostle Paul's frustration in Romans chapter 7. Obviously, Paul understood his co-crucifixion with Christ and his new nature, because he had just written Romans chapter 6; but here we find him in defeat, why? Paul is feeling the struggle between the flesh and the spirit. Our flesh still wants life to go on like it did before we were born again. It is still striving to get us to react as if we are not new creations (II Corinthians 5:17). It is still striving to be in control. On the other hand, we desire to do God's will in our inner man, which was "created in Christ Jesus for good works" (Ephesians 2:10).

If we try to perform what our spirit man wants to do in our own strength, our flesh will be in control, and we will not be able to do that which we want to do.

Only as we rely in compete dependence on the life of Christ within us can we do that which we want to do. Only when we know we are totally accepted by God because of what Jesus did and not by what we do can we cease from our own works and enter into His rest (Hebrew 4:10).

This is the battle we feel within us, the struggle for rule. There is a constant tug of war between the flesh and the spirit. Remember diagram 2.3. The more of the flesh that is renewed, the less flesh there is left to pull against the spirit. It does get easier!

Personal Study

Meditate on who or what your life revolves around. Who or what is at the center of your life? Be honest with yourself and write this in the center of the wheel below. Next, write in the names of the people or things that make up the "spokes" in your life.

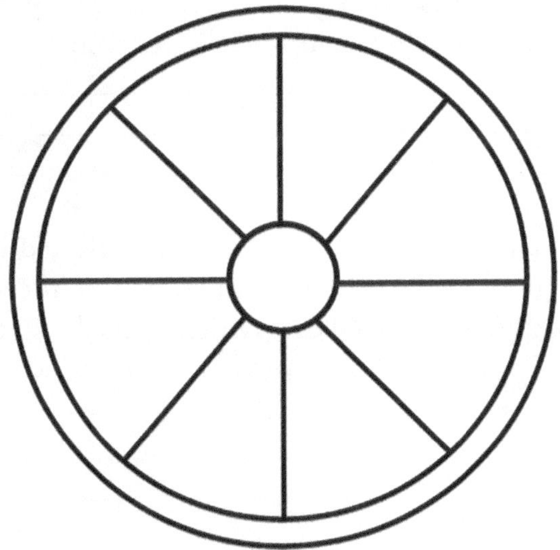

If you are having difficulty identifying the center, try this test: imagine laying the spokes of your life on an altar like Abraham did to Isaac. (Remember, the spokes of your life can be family members, your reputation, your job, your ministry, your health, comfort, etc.) Then, think what your response would be if any one or all of the spokes were removed or taken from your life. If you could not imagine going on with life without one or more of the "spokes" you wrote down, this (these) is (are) the center of your life.

1. Meditate on your physical, mental, and emotional condition. Are you showing signs of excessive wear? Remember, wear comes from an unbalanced life that does not revolve around Jesus.

    ____

    ____

    ____

2. Look up Galatians 5:22–23. What are the nine facets of the fruit of the Spirit? These are the characteristics that will be brought forth in your life when your life revolves around Jesus.

    ____

    ____

    ____

3. Read Romans 12:1–2. A living sacrifice referred to an animal that was given to the priests to rend service to them all the days of its life and was not killed as other animal sacrifices. That is what the Lord asks of us, to yield ourselves for whatever use He has for us, all the days of our life.

    ____

    ____

    ____

CHAPTER 8

Hindrances to Holiness (Wholeness) Healing of the Brokenhearted

You now have thoroughly studied who you are since Jesus exchanged His nature for your old nature. You have also been challenged with the necessity of complete dependence on and surrender to the life of Christ within you. As you "consider yourself dead to sin but alive to God" (Romans 6:11) and yield control of your life continually to Christ, you should begin to change from the inside out.

There are three areas that repeatedly seem to hinder Christians from walking victoriously. In the next three chapters, we will examine these hindrances. Don't become introspective, but if the Holy Spirit reveals an area of unrest, deal with it now. The Lord is faithful to continually arrange the circumstances of our lives so our weak areas are exposed to His searchlight. If we don't choose to repent of the weakness of the flesh that God reveals, He will continue to bring the same weakness to the surface until we choose to change. If we continually refuse to deal with what the Holy Spirit is revealing to us, our hearts will start to harden. If we allow our hearts to harden, we will be on very dangerous ground. The more we harden our heart, the greater the circumstances must be to bring us to the point of desperation and the more "death" we will reap. The sooner we repent and consider ourselves dead to any trace of our self-life, the easier the process is. As you study these next three chapters, I challenge you to surrender every area of "self-control" in your life.

The first area we are going to discuss may not seem like self-centeredness. Many people who have been victimized and deeply wounded feel they have nothing to deal with because what happened was not their fault. This could certainly be true, but once the truth of Jesus as the healer of the brokenhearted is revealed to you, you are responsible for the choice to allow Him to heal you or to remain broken and impaired. If you choose not to change, you are allowing self to remain in control of your life. In Luke 4:18 of the KJV of the bible, Jesus said:

> The Spirit of the Lord is upon me, because He hath anointed me to preach the gospel to the poor; He hath sent me to heal the brokenhearted, to preach deliverance to the captives, and recovering of sight to the blind, to set at liberty them that are bruised. (Luke 4:18 (KJV))

Jesus bore in His body our grief, our sorrow, our pain from incest or abuse, our rejection, our shame, or any other infirmity we have ever experienced. He carried these to the cross so we would not have to bear them—what love!

> Surely our griefs He Himself bore and our sorrows He carried; yet we ourselves esteemed Him stricken, smitten of God, and afflicted. But He was pierced through for our transgressions, He was crushed for our iniquities; The chastening for our well-being fell upon Him, and by His scourging we are healed. (Isaiah 53:4–5)

The sacrificial death on the cross that shed sinless blood for our sins, the exchange that took our old nature to the cross with Jesus and gave us His nature, is the same work that took our grief, pain, and sorrows to the cross, once and for all. Jesus bore our sin and sickness. He died so we might exchange all that is broken in our hearts for peace, joy, contentment, gratefulness, and all that He is. He died that we might have life more abundantly, and we cannot experience abundant life with a broken heart.

How do we know if we have a broken heart, and how does it affect us? There are actually two areas of our being that can suffer from brokenness. The first is in the soul, and the second is in the human spirit. It is not necessary to determine where the wound is for healing, but an awareness of the two possibilities is helpful.

Let us first examine the effects of a broken heart. We studied in earlier chapters about the fact of our bodies and souls being the vessels of the treasure of the Holy Spirt (Diagram 2.4). Our soul encompasses our spirit, which is made up of the Holy Spirit joined to our human spirit. Envision diagram 2.4, with many cracks and even holes in it. As the Lord pours in His grace—the power and desire to do His will—into the vessel through the Holy Spirit, the "oil" of the Spirit leaks out as fast as it is being poured in. Psalm 31:9–12 gives us a picture of a broken vessel.

> Be gracious to me, O Lord, for I am in distress; My eye is wasted away from grief, my soul and my body also. For my life is spent with sorrow, and my years with sighing; My strength has failed because of my iniquity, and my body has wasted away. Because of all my adversaries, I have become a reproach, especially to my neighbors, and an object of dread to my acquaintances; those who see me in the street flee from me. I am forgotten as a dead man, out of mind, I am like a broken vessel. (Psalm 31:9–12)

I am sure you have known Christians, maybe even yourself, who seem to grow very little despite the abundance of good biblical teaching and adherence to sound Christian disciplines. A person with a broken heart will usually grow very little and very slowly.

Do not confuse the brokenness of the mind and emotions we are speaking of here with the needful breaking of the will we discussed in chapter 4. The will must be broken of its confidence in the flesh so it can be totally dependent on the spirit. When the will is broken, it will gladly choose the spirit as the power source for the soul (Diagram 2.5). When the will is broken, the oil of the Spirit within will be released to a lost and dying world. When the mind or emotions are broken, the treasure the will is choosing to release from the spirit leaks out as it flows through the soul, in proportion to the degree of brokenness (Diagram 8.1). Consequently, the grace needed to grow is not contained within the vessel, and the tug of war with the flesh will often be lost.

Diagram 8.1

The flow of the 'oil' of the Spirit in the Brokenhearted.

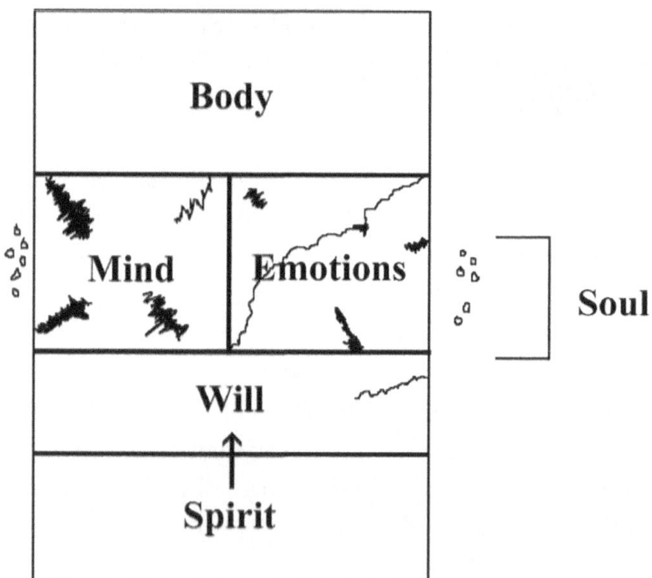

The other place brokenness can occur is in the human spirit. Brokenness in the human spirit can affect us in much the same way as in the soul, but the spiritual dynamics are different. Scripture gives us several examples of the effects of a wounded spirit.

A joyful heart is good medicine. But a broken spirit
dries up the bones. (Proverbs 17:22)

The spirit of a man can endure his sickness. But a
broken spirit who can bear? (Proverbs 18:14)

A joyful heart makes a cheerful face. But when the
heart is sad, the spirit is broken. (Proverbs 15:13)

In order to understand the dynamics of a wounded spirit, let's
review what happened to our human spirit when we were born again.
Scripture tells us the Holy Spirit joined our human spirit, giving it
life. It was not our human spirit that was crucified with Christ; it was
our old nature. The human spirit, then, is given life by its union with
the Holy Spirit, but not replaced. Romans chapter 8 verse 16 shows
us the existence of the human spirit after regeneration: "The Spirit
Himself bears witness with our spirit that we are children of God."

Sometimes, the wounds from the events in our lives are so deep
and so traumatic they reach all the way to our human spirit. When
the human spirit is wounded, it reacts like a physical wound that
never heals properly. If you had a broken leg when you were young
and it was never properly set, you would probably walk with a limp
for the rest of your life. If stress was applied to that area, it might even
hurt years after the original wound. Since the Holy Spirit is joined
to the human spirit, brokenness in the human spirit will impede the
flow of the Holy Spirit in our lives (Diagram 8.2).

Diagram 8.2

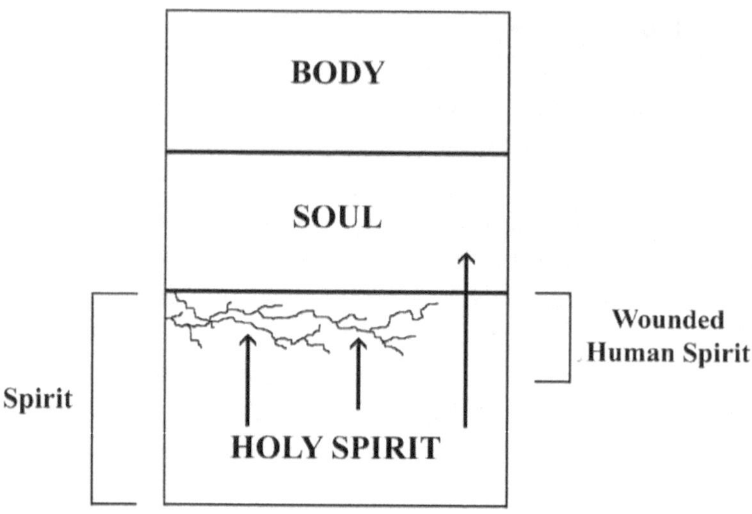

It is important to understand the effects of brokenness so we might recognize our need and turn to Jesus as the Healer of our broken heart. Just as we do not want to get off-balance and become introspective, we also do not want to ignore the signs of a broken heart, whether in the soul or in the human spirit.

One of the major signs of brokenness is oversensitivity in a certain area. For example, if you have suffered much rejection in your life, then until you are healed, you will be prone to feeling rejected—whether real or imaginary. For instance, if a friend leaves a room without saying goodbye, you feel rejected. You might even be sure the friend is mad at you. Numerous thoughts will torment your mind for hours. This would be an overreaction to the situation presented. Eventually, you could allow yourself to get so paranoid; your friends really would start to avoid you because your paranoia would drive them crazy. When your behavior is irrational or is an overreaction to reality, brokenness in that area is often the cause.

Another symptom of a broken heart is emotional pain when a situation similar to a painful past experience is mentioned. For example, if your father abandoned your family when you were young, any situation where you would fear being left alone could cause negative emotions to rise up within you. Whether the subject triggers fear or shame, pain, or guilt, the heart is likely broken if negative emotions are aroused.

The third area in which brokenness surfaces is the inability to function in the broken area. If your heart was broken due to poverty as a child, it is possible you will not handle the money you do have wisely and will never seem to be able to succeed financially. It is almost as if money pours out your "cracks" faster than it comes in (Diagram 8.1 and 8.2).

Another example of the inability to function could be in getting up in front of people. If you were humiliated in earlier years while attempting to speak in front of an audience, your broken heart could disable your attempts to overcome this fear, even if you really do desire to speak in public. A general guideline of determining brokenness is this—Jesus died to give you His life so you could have abundant life. When you are not experiencing abundant life (all that Jesus is) in any particular area, either you are walking after the flesh or you are brokenhearted. If you are not sure which of these is at the root of your overreaction or negative emotions, ask the Lord. He is faithful to perfect that which concerns you and to finish the work He has begun (Psalm 138:8, Philippians 1:6).

We can be so thankful we do not have to live with the wounds an imperfect world has given us. Jesus bore every one of these wounds in His body on the cross that we might not have to bear them.

> The Lord is near to the brokenhearted, and saves those who are crushed in spirit. (Psalm 34:18)

> He heals the brokenhearted, and binds up their wounds. (Psalm 147:3)

Today, by faith, you can give any negative emotion you are carrying to Jesus and let Him give you peace, joy, and contentment in return. You may still be able to remember the incidents that left you wounded, but when Jesus heals, the pain will be gone. Jesus has already paid the price, but you must believe it and let the past go. You must want to be healed more than you want pity, or the comfort zone of the familiar. Jesus died that you might be completely free. Don't waste what He has done for you!

Personal Study

1. What four things did Jesus bear in His body on the cross?

2. What is the difference between brokenness of the mind and emotions and the breaking of the will?

3. What are the two parts of a human being that can suffer from brokenness?

4. What effect does the brokenness of the mind and emotions have on a person?

5. What are three major signs of brokeness?

CHAPTER 9

Hindrances to Holiness (Wholeness) The Crippling Effect of Unforgiveness

The second area that cripples much of the Body of Christ is unforgiveness. There is much talk about forgiveness. However, most people do not understand how to walk it out and most are fooled by their flesh. Eventually, the hope of ever being free from the hatred and bitterness inside is lost. Having tried over and over again to "forgive," they resign themselves to the fact the "ought" against them was greater than anyone else can understand. They feel they are destined or have a "right" to remain in unforgiveness. If Jesus, who was without sin, died for the forgiveness of the worst sinner, then through His power, we can forgive all who have hurt us.

> But He, having offered one sacrifice for sins for all time,
> sat down at the right hand of God. (Hebrews 10:12)

> I can do all things through Him who strengthens me.
> (Philippians 4:13)

As we have studied in previous chapters, our will is the part of us that chooses whether to plug into the power of the spirit or of the flesh. In the next few pages, we will be studying scriptures that make it clear that if we want abundant life we must forgive everyone for everything. Since we clearly know the will of God is to forgive, choosing to forgive is yielding to the spirit. Thus, we need to review the process of yielding to the spirit and the common reaction of our flesh to that choice.

The first step in walking after the spirit is determining the will of God. The Holy Spirit guides us according to God's will. We then have a choice whether or not to follow the leading of the Holy Spirit. If we choose to yield to the Spirit the power of God will be released through our soul, giving the body the signal it needs to perform God's will. If we need to forgive someone, since we know it is God's will, yielding to the spirit will let the forgiveness of Jesus flow through us.

As an act of our will, we have then chosen to forgive no matter how we feel. In fact, until our emotions are greatly renewed in this area, most likely we will feel no different, even after making the choice to forgive. This is where many are tripped up. Forgiveness works just like any other fruit of the Spirit we need to see manifested in our lives. We recognize the need for change in our attitudes or actions. We know our sinful nature was crucified with Christ and we now have His nature. We know that, in Jesus, we have all we need for life and godliness. Finally, we know that when we allow Christ to be in control of our lives, we will experience His life in our bodies. As we yield to Jesus to produce His life in us (in this case, forgiveness), the attribute we need will begin to come forth in our attitudes and actions.

Meanwhile, our flesh does not want to lose control, so it will manifest in our minds and emotions to make us think applying the truth of the exchanged life does not work. We may even feel more hatred and bitterness than before we challenged the flesh. Remember, the flesh lost its authority to rule over us when our old man was crucified with Christ, but it will bluff us to see if we know it has lost its power. If we stand firm in our faith in the word of God, eventually the flesh will give up, and an area of our flesh is then renewed. Sometimes, we will feel instant relief; sometimes, it can take years. However, once an area of flesh is renewed, there is less to tug on the flesh's side of the tug of war (Diagram 2.3), and the tug of war is more easily won by the spirit. Do not get discouraged in well doing; this is a very gradual process!

In order to take a stand against our flesh, we must know God definitely wants us to forgive any wrong done to us. Otherwise, when our flesh comes against our spirit, we will back down and rationalize our situation is so bad we can't be expected to forgive.

One of the places in scripture where the Lord makes the need for forgiveness very clear is in Matthew 18: 21–35. In this passage, Peter asks Jesus how often he must forgive. You will notice Peter does not yet understand the heart of God, but is looking for a rule to keep in order for the law to be fulfilled. Knowing this, Jesus' reply takes Peter by surprise. Instead of being impressed with Peter's offer to forgive an offender seven times, Jesus states that His standard is forgiving seventy times seven. This implied that Peter, who is representative of God's will for us, was to forgive as often as he was offended. Then Jesus tells Peter this parable explaining the principle of forgiveness (paraphrase from Matthew 18):

A certain king had a slave who owed him more than the slave could possibly pay back in a lifetime. So the king orders the slave and his family to be sold as payment toward the indebtedness. The slave pleads with the king to have mercy on him and the king, moved with compassion, forgives the debt. The parable then proceeds to say, the same slave that was forgiven a debt he could never have paid goes to another slave who owes him only a day's wage and demands payment. Unlike the merciful king, the forgiven slave has the second slave thrown into prison until the debt is satisfied. When other slaves hear of what the forgiven slave did to the one who owed him only a day's wage, they went and told the king. The outraged king sends for the slave whom he had forgiven and releases him to the torturers until the debt was paid. After telling Peter this parable, Jesus then states His Heavenly Father will do the same to anyone who will not forgive an offender from their heart (Matthew 18:21-35).

In this parable, God is conveying the need to always forgive. Despite what wrong has been done to you—no matter how hideous—God is saying you must forgive. God would not tell us to do something that we do not have the power to do. We must believe we do have the power through Christ Jesus. The same power that raised Jesus from the dead resides in every believer. This is the actual life of God, who loved us even while we were sinners. In God's eyes, one sin is not greater than another. If we have transgressed the law in one point, we are guilty in all points (James 2:10). In other words, you and I are just as guilty in God's eyes as the worst sexual deviant, mass murderer, or person involved in human trafficking. Apart from God's grace, they deserve only eternity in hell, but apart from His grace, so do you and I.

In order to understand the parable in Matthew 18, we must comprehend what we have been forgiven of. We have been forgiven of a debt we could never pay by the King of Kings. Since "all of our righteousness is as filthy rags" (Isaiah 64:6), we have no more hope of forgiveness than the "worst" sinner. No matter how good we are in our own eyes, as compared to the "mass murderer," we too "have fallen short of the glory of God" (Romans 3:23).

God's standard is His righteousness, as seen in Jesus, and all of us have fallen short of His standard. Since God has forgiven us a debt we could never have paid, then the least we can do is to forgive all those who have offended us. Otherwise, God will turn us over to the "torturers."

Exactly who or what are the torturers? There are several schools of thought, and they may all be correct. The torturers may actually be demonic spirits that God allows to have access to us when we refuse to forgive. They could be spirits such as hatred, bitterness, envy, depression, or infirmity. These demonic forces will rob us of the abundant life that Jesus died to give us. Our lack of forgiveness will not harm the one who we will not release from prison, but unforgiveness will make us miserable. We will never have peace until we choose to forgive from our heart.

The torturers may also be the physical symptoms that even medical doctors know are caused by unforgiveness, symptoms, which include headaches, nervous tension, numerous stomach disorders, some forms of arthritis, or skin rashes. Whenever the flesh is in control of our lives, rather than Christ, we will suffer adverse reactions in our soulish realm, and the soulish realm always affects the physical.

> Beloved, I pray that in all respects you may prosper
> and be in good health even as your soul prospers.
> (III John 1:2)

The last area in which we will suffer from unforgiveness is a basic law of the kingdom. If we sow to the flesh (which is what we are doing if we refuse to forgive), from the flesh, we will reap corruption (Galatians 6:8). Now corruption is everything contrary to abundant life. If we plant fleshly seeds through unforgiveness, we will reap trouble in this life. The rain does fall on the just and the unjust, but when we sow to the flesh, Satan has God's permission to bring us a harvest from what we have sown. God has made His laws of life on this earth very clear—so that in wisdom—we might be blessed. On the contrary, if we ignore the laws of the kingdom, we will suffer unnecessarily in this life. Until we ask God to forgive us for our unforgiveness towards men, we will continue to reap a crop of decay and ruin.

> Do not be deceived, God is not mocked; for whatever
> a man sows, this he will also reap. (Galatians 6:7)

Another principle of sowing to the flesh, in this case, unforgiveness, is you become the slave of the one to whom you present or yield yourself to. If you allow yourself to continue in unforgiveness, which is flesh, then you will become a slave of the flesh, resulting in further *"lawlessness."*

Walking in the known sin of unforgiveness will dwarf our spiritual growth and give our flesh an open door to enslave us in other areas of our lives. No matter what the offense was or is, unforgiveness is not worth it!

> Do you not know that when you present yourselves
> to someone as slaves for obedience, you are slaves of
> the one who you obey, either of sin resulting in death,
> or of obedience resulting in righteousness? But thanks
> be to God that though you were slaves of sin, you

> became obedient from the heart to that form of teach-
> ing to which you were committed, and having been
> freed from sin, you became slaves of righteousness. I
> am speaking in human terms because of the weakness
> of your flesh. For just as you presented your mem-
> bers as slaves to impurity and to lawlessness, resulting
> in further lawlessness, so now present your members
> as slaves to righteousness, resulting in sanctification.
> (Romans 6:16–19)

The next question you might be pondering is why is it so hard to forgive? The very root of unforgiveness is our own "selves" demand for control. The flesh or self is self-centered and wants everything and everyone to revolve around it. When someone has offended us, we think we have the right to get even or to make them pay for what they did. At best, we are at least going to hold it over their heads. Do you see the root? The root is control. We want to control the situation so we can demand what we want for what was done to us. If we were to forgive, the person who offended us would be released from our control and our resulting demands. We may even want to control our life to such an extent that we are even denying anything ever happened. Refusing to face reality will never change the truth. Only by accepting what has happened can we receive the supernatural power of God to forgive and be set free.

Remember, as a free gift, the King has forgiven us of all we have ever done or will ever do and He expects us to do the same. Our demand for revenge will not make the offender nearly as miserable as ourselves. We may originally have been the victim, but if we choose not to forgive, we are now the one who is guilty. The weeks, months, or years of torment—after seeing the need for forgiveness—are our fault, not the original offender's. Jesus died for us so He could live in us, to give us the power to forgive and be free. The choice is yours.

There is another very important point that must be made. Biblical forgiveness is not done through "willpower" or because you're the "better person." Most religions teach forgiveness and even atheists forgive based on what could be called a subtle, "one-upmanship."

Such motives including "I will return good where others have been bad," "I will take the higher road," "I will just try to forget about it and go on," or "I will excuse them" are not sufficient. Biblical forgiveness is based only on the shed blood of Jesus Christ.

Jesus humbled Himself to come to this earth in the form of a man—a human being. He then lived away from the Father and His heavenly home for thirty-three years on an earth and with a people cursed from sin. Ultimately, He submitted Himself to torture and suffered a horrific death on the cross. His blood was willingly shed in our place, for according to the law, "all things are cleansed with blood, and without shedding of blood there is no forgiveness" (Hebrews 9:22b). Whether we like it or not, the *shedding of blood* is God's requirement for forgiveness, and Jesus freely did this out of love for us.

With this is mind, the choice to forgive is still yours, but the decision must be made in the framework of the blood of a sinless Savior being shed for the forgiveness of our sins.

> He made Him who knew no sin to be sin on our
> behalf, so that we might become the righteousness of
> God in Him. (II Corinthians 5:21)

Once again, since Jesus forgave everything we have ever done or will ever do, we are commanded to forgive every offense against us: past, present, and future. Let's take a look at the forgiveness process again from a slightly different perspective.

The first step is prerequisite to any victory over the flesh:

Give up—admit you can't forgive the person in your own strength—and cry out to God for His help, which is grace. One definition of grace is the desire and power to do God's will. Even if you do not desire to forgive (but know God expects you to and that you will be miserable if you do not), cry out for God's grace—for the desire to do His will. Biblical forgiveness is based on the shed blood of Jesus Christ.

The next step is also always necessary to remember when dealing with the flesh:

Your will must choose to yield to the spirit or in this case, forgive, before you will ever feel like it. We must again consider the battle between the flesh and the spirit. As an act of our will, we choose to obey the spirit, which in this chapter, is to forgive. When the will chooses the spirit as the power source (review Diagram 2.3), the power of the Holy Spirit will flow through the soul, resulting in the eventual renewing of the emotions in order to feel forgiveness. The period between the choice and the feelings is the "fight of faith" (I Timothy 6:12). Will you believe the truth about *"Christ in you"* being "the hope of glory" (Colossians 1:27), glory being the character of God, or will you go by what you think or feel? Faith believes in what we cannot perceive with our five senses.

The last step is based on God's example:

Choose to "remember no more!" The Lord declares in Jeremiah 31:34b, "for I will forgive their iniquity, and their sin I will remember no more." I cannot believe that an omniscient, all knowing God, gets amnesia. So how does God forget? He chooses not to bring our sins to mind, to remember them no more. We must also choose not to allow any thoughts of offenses against us in our minds. Our flesh, in league with Satan, will repeatedly bring the memories before us. Again, our response must come from our will, not our mind or emotions. If we do not allow ourselves to even think about past offenses, let alone speak of them, nor allow others to bring them to mind, eventually the memory will fade. Whenever an offense is flashed before us, we remind the flesh that we have chosen to forgive, and we are not taking the offense back. The power of the flesh to antagonize us into unforgiveness will gradually weaken until we can hardly even "try" to remember the incident.

The Lord's power to heal our broken hearts must work hand in hand with forgiveness. Unless our hearts are healed from the wounds of the offense, it will be very difficult to forgive.

We can be free from the offenses of the past that haunt us. However, we must admit we cannot forgive in our own strength. As an act of our will, we must decide to forgive, until the feelings come, no matter how long that takes. Then we must choose to never think, listen, or speak of them again.

We can walk in a lifestyle of continual forgiveness. Offenses are guaranteed to come in this life. How we deal with them is the key to abundant living. When we are offended, we must ask the Lord to heal the hurt and choose to forgive. If we will not let offenses take root, or share them with others, we will truly begin to get a glimpse of being like our Father, Who is in heaven.

Jesus is saying to you today:

- I am <u>not</u> saying they were not wrong.
- I am <u>not</u> saying you were not hurt.
- I <u>am saying</u> I paid the price!

Personal Study

1. Read Matthew 18:21–35.

2. Study Luke 15:11–12. The elder brother could not forgive because of his own self-righteousness. He had been serving the Father out of duty—not love. Sometimes, it is easy to forget what we were like before Christ, what we deserve from a holy God, and where we would be apart from grace.

3. Study Luke 17:1–10.

4. In Psalm 55:12–14, read David's account of the special hurt from offenses from those closest to us. Remember, all human beings are capable of walking after the flesh. Whether parents, church leaders, or others we admire, we all have to battle against the desire of our flesh. We cannot expect more from others than God does from us. By the standard that we judge, we will be judged.

5. Complete, with an attitude of prayer; Appendix II, My Action Plan to Forgive. Share your results with a trusted friend, who can hold you accountable and pray with you and for you, as you work your way through your "action plan."

CHAPTER 10

Hindrances to Holiness (Wholeness) The Paralyzing Effect of People Pleasing

> Nevertheless, many even of the rulers believed in Him, but because of the Pharisees they were not confessing Him, lest they should be put out of the synagogue; for they loved the approval of men rather than the approval of God. (John 12:42–43)

Does the approval of men mean more to you than the approval of God? You might very religiously answer no, but pay attention to how you react the next time you fear the disapproval of those around you. Wait for the feeling of paralysis and take note of your hesitation. The fear of men is a very powerful force.

From the time we are young children, we learn not to do certain things or the other kids will laugh at us. We are taught to make sure our clothes match and to have no holes in our socks, not nearly so much from a good grooming standpoint, but so we will be accepted by our peers.

We also know how those who are "a little different" are treated. They are ridiculed, called painful names, chosen last for any team, and rejected from the "in crowd." We learn our lessons well: "fit in," "don't make waves," and act and look like everyone else in order to avoid the pain of rejection.

The fear of rejection is a controlling force in our lives, but since it doesn't interfere with "normal living," it is almost undetected as a significant foe in the Body of Christ.

> How can you believe, when you receive glory from
> one another, and you do not seek the glory that is
> from the one and only God? (John 5:44)

We might expect the world to be controlled by "people pleasing" since everyone has a deep desire to be accepted, and the world does not know the love and acceptance of God through Jesus Christ. Sadly enough—even knowing the truth—most of the Body of Christ does not really feel accepted by God through the finished work of Christ. Consequently, most Christians are just as bound by the fear of rejection as the world; but even sadder yet is the fact that much of the time, it is the fear of rejection by their own brothers and sisters in Christ. Home should be a place of love and security, and the church body you call "home" should be the last place you would ever have to fear rejection.

The problem is the majority of the church of Jesus Christ tends to follow a form of religion rather than the "simplicity and purity of devotion to Christ" (II Corinthians 11:3b). If we follow our head, which is Jesus, then His unconditional love will be expressed through us to others. There is no rejection imparted from unconditional love. This does not mean a setting aside of biblical standards, but an acceptance of who a person is, as well as where they have come from. As we concentrate on desiring to "love our neighbor as ourselves" (Matthew 22:39), through the strength of Christ, rejection will gradually be replaced by love.

When we concentrate on outward behavior, anyone who does not have the same list of standards as we do is rejected as "ungodly." We can then easily become self-righteous from our "keeping the list of dos and don'ts" and forget what we are really like, or would be, apart from Christ. We are only "dirt," earthen vessels containing the treasure (II Corinthians 4:7), which is Christ. We came from dust, and our earthly tents will return to dust. When we become self-righteous and condemning, we reject those who Jesus died for. We are then no different from the world, accepting those who act like we want them to and rejecting those who dare to let us see what they are really like.

How can this monster be overcome? We must become so secure in God's acceptance of us that the deep need in our hearts for love and acceptance is fulfilled in Christ, not by the people around us. This does not mean we do not desire love and acceptance from others, but that we are so secure and content in God's love and acceptance we can be happy without receiving it from others. To arrive at this place is truly supernatural, but we have the life of our supernatural God living in us.

Since the flesh was programmed to think and feel like the "natural man," it craves acceptance from people and is totally controlled by either their acceptance or the fear of their rejection. Since we are no longer in the flesh, but in the Spirit, we can consider ourselves dead to the need for man's approval, but alive to God's approval (Romans 6:11). In other words, as we choose death to the need for the approval of men and trust in God's total acceptance of us through Jesus Christ, our flesh will be renewed from "glory to glory" (II Corinthians 3:18), and we will move toward freedom.

In order to trust in God's acceptance of us, we must renew our minds to what God's word says about our status as believers. Ephesians 1:6 (NKJV) tells us, "to the praise of the glory of His grace, by which He made us accepted in the Beloved." This verse states that by God's grace, we are accepted in the *Beloved,* which is in the Body of Christ. Using the definition of grace of, "unmerited favor;" we are accepted by God as His beloved by no merit of our own. We did not do anything to be accepted by God in the first place, and nothing we can do or not do will be the basis for His continued acceptance of us. God's love is unconditional. This means we cannot earn His acceptance nor cause Him to reject us. If we could, then we would not be accepted by His grace, but our acceptance would be earned.

> Now to the one who works, his wage is not reckoned
> as a favor but what is due. (Romans 4:4)

Romans 6:23 tells us, "the wages of sin is death." That is, death is what we deserve, no matter how good we are. The verse then goes on to tell us, "but the gift of God is eternal life through Jesus Christ our Lord."

Eternal life is synonymous with Christ's life, so God's gift to us is Christ's life. If you were given a box full of items as a gift, everything in that box would be yours. Scripture tells us that "everything pertaining to life and godliness" (II Peter 1:3) is ours through Christ Jesus. So when we received God's gift of eternal life, we received all that Jesus is. How acceptable to God the Father is Jesus? God Himself spoke from heaven and declared, "This is my beloved Son in whom I am well pleased" (Matthew 3:17).

Why is Jesus accepted by a righteous Father? Jesus is accepted because He is totally righteous. When we received Jesus as a gift from God, we received all that Jesus is not because we deserve it, but by God's grace—His unmerited favor.

> He made Him who knew no sin to be sin on our
> behalf, that we might become the righteousness of
> God in Him. (II Corinthians 5:21)

We do not become God, but we do become "partakers of the divine nature." (II Peter 1:4)

> But by His doing you are in Christ Jesus, who became
> to us wisdom from God, and righteousness and sanc-
> tification, and redemption. (I Corinthians 1:30)

By renewing our minds to God's total acceptance of us, because of "Christ who is our life" (Colossians 3:4), we can become fulfilled in God's love and acceptance. This will free us from the approval of men.

> For am I now seeking the favor of men, or of God?
> Or am I striving to please men? If I were still trying to
> please men, I would not be a bond-servant of Christ.
> (Galatians 1:10)

When we were born again, we became children of God. From the time of that new birth, Jehovah began to arrange the circumstances of our lives to bring us to mature sons and daughters. Our Heavenly Father gives us the freedom to walk after the flesh or after the spirit but draws us unto Himself, hoping we will desire intimacy with Him. He gives us a revelation of His uncompromising love for us, hoping that our response to His love will be such a compelling love on our part we will lay down our lives for Him.

If we really long to do His will, we will yield our will—our lives totally to Him. We will choose to be a bond servant of Christ. In biblical times, a bond servant was a servant who was given the chance to be free but chose to serve the master out of love. The servant's ear was then pierced with an awl, as a sign of voluntary servitude for the rest of his life. We will never be all God purposed us to be if we are not willing to go beyond childhood to maturity. When our love for Jesus can no longer allow us to live apart from Him, we will pay the price of becoming a bond servant. Being a bond servant is not always easy, but will be the only road our hearts will allow us to take.

A bond servant has chosen to give up his own rights to serve the master. He willingly lives as a living sacrifice (Romans 12:1), because love will allow nothing less. A bond servant's duty is only to serve and please his master. When we are striving to please those around us, including our family, then the motivating force in our life is not the fulfillment of our Master's desire. When we are controlled by the opinions of people, we cannot walk victoriously.

> But seek first His kingdom and His righteousness; and
> all these things shall be added to you. (Matthew 6:33)

Three Hindrances to Holiness

There are three subtle areas through which the longing for the approval of men works to control us. If the approval of others controls us, then the Spirit of God cannot. Scripture clearly tells us to be filled or controlled by the Spirit (Ephesians 5:18). The deception is subtle and deadly.

The first area the enemy of our souls uses to control us is concern for our reputation. After all, no one wants to be thought of in a negative way. As long as we worry about what someone else thinks about us and allow that concern to motivate our thoughts and actions, we are being controlled by that person. I am not suggesting an attitude of, "I could care less," in regard to those around us—that would not be love. However, there is a need to be honest with ourselves as to the motives of our hearts in the decisions we make and the words we speak. Jesus was our example on this earth, of how a man, surrendered to the Spirit of God, should walk. Jesus Himself, even though he was God, walked in total humility and was not concerned with His reputation.

> Have this attitude in yourselves which was also in Christ Jesus, who, although He existed in the form of God, did not regard equality with God a thing to be grasped, but emptied Himself [7] taking the form of a bond servant, and being made in the likeness of men. (Philippians 2:5–7)

The second tactic the enemy uses for control is combining the fear of rejection with concern for our reputation. We touched on this earlier in the chapter. We learn how to be accepted and how to avoid rejection at an early age. It is very easy to learn since the pain of rejection is very real. Rejection is like an electric fence. Even a cow knows

---

[7] "Emptied Himself" actually means "laid aside His privileges" (Harper Study Bible, New American Standard, copyright 1985 by the Zondervan Corp). When we humble ourselves, we give up our rights, choose death to our concern for our reputation, and lay aside our privileges for the sake of the gospel.

that if it goes beyond the acceptable boundaries, it is going to feel a jolt of pain from the fence. The fear of the pain of rejection keeps us within the acceptable boundaries of those around us. We also learn how to build barriers, called "walls," to protect ourselves from future hurt. The problem is the walls we build also keep us from going to Jesus, who is the only source of healing for our rejection. This pattern can be destructive. The more we are rejected, the more walls we build, which keep us from the only hope of freedom, who is Jesus. Jesus never goes away from us, but we hide inside our self-built fortresses, afraid of letting even Jesus touch us.

One last area Satan uses to control us is almost unknown as a spiritual force. This deadly form of control is codependency. Codependency is having someone other than Christ as the center of our life. An outstanding example of this is the mindset held by a large number of women, of their self-worth being dependent on the man they have in their lives. Women are not exclusive in their codependency, but scripture has something very specific to say to women bound by people pleasing. Women are taught at a young age that having a boyfriend makes them a desirable person. If by the time they get to their high school prom and don't have a date, then there definitely must be something wrong with them. What a contrast to the truth of God's acceptance and love in Christ. Jesus is the only One we can be addicted to. If we are addicted to anyone else, we have no hope of abundant life.

Genesis 3:16 records the curse on Eve and all her female descendants for partaking of the Tree of the Knowledge of Good and Evil. The last part of the verse reads, "Yet your desire shall be for your husband and he shall rule over you." Until the Lord revealed to me what the curse really was, I could not understand why *desire* for your husband was a curse, when the New Testament clearly teaches women to love and reverence their husbands. I have heard teaching that states this verse means a woman should have to do everything her husband desires. If that were the case, that would just be another way of stating the husband would rule over the wife. Genesis 3:16 seems to be stating two different, but related, ideas. I then asked the Lord for understanding and studied the word "desire," which seemed to be the key to correct interpretation. *Strong's Concordance* lists the meaning of the original word for *desire* as "a stretching out after, a longing." Again, a healthy longing for your husband is not a curse. So what is the Bible saying? This desire is a craving for a woman's emotional needs to be met, which will never be satisfied by a human being. Since this craving is never fulfilled, the woman will do anything for the love and approval of her man, and consequently, he will rule over her. This curse of never ending desire will possess a woman, and she will return repeatedly, even to an abusive situation for her "fix." Rather than being addicted to Jesus, she is addicted to a man. This is the curse spoken of in Genesis 3:16.

Christ redeemed us from the curse of the law, because He became a curse for us: "Cursed is everyone who hangs on a tree" (Galatians 3:13). All the curses ever spoken on mankind, all the curses resulting from disobedience to the law, were laid on Jesus for our freedom. A woman will never be free until she realizes Jesus is the only One who will ever satisfy all her emotional needs. When this becomes a reality, she can quit making demands on her husband that he cannot fulfill. She can stop trying to control her circumstances to get her needs met and trust Jesus to fulfill the desires of her heart. A woman who has not allowed Jesus to set her free from the curse in Genesis 3:16 is the contentious woman spoken of in Proverbs 25:24. She is the woman who is so demanding and hard to live with it would be better to live on a housetop alone than with her.

When you realize Jesus can fulfill your deepest needs, you can be set free from the curse, and your man will not control you because of your addiction. Instead, you will be free to gladly submit to your husband for Christ's sake. Since you have already given all your rights to Jesus and all authority is established by God (Romans 13:1), submitting to your husband is submitting to Christ. This is not a punishment because of Eve's disobedience. God's order of functional authority—first Adam was formed, then Eve—was already established before the fall.

In Christ, there is neither male nor female, but one Spirit. The same Spirit that raised Jesus from the dead lives in redeemed men and women alike. Godly women can walk in the freedom that Christ died to give them—free to love, free to serve, and free to submit.

Whether male or female, you will never be free to be all that Christ has for you until you are set free from the control of people pleasing. "It was for freedom that Christ set us free" (Galatians 5:1a). Don't put yourself back under the tyranny of another's approval, but walk in freedom. Until you choose death to your flesh's desire for a good reputation, until you refuse to let the fear of rejection control you, and until you are addicted to no one but Jesus, the life of Christ will be greatly hindered from being displayed in your life. Jesus died so you could be *free indeed*, which is completely free!

> If therefore the Son shall make you free, you shall be free indeed. (John 8:36)

Personal Study

1. What are your flesh's attempts to be approved by others?

   ____

   ____

   ____

2. When you received the gift of eternal life (Jesus), what was included in the box?

   ____

   ____

   ____

3. What is a bond servant?

   ____

   ____

   ____

4. What are the three major areas of "people pleasing" that the enemy uses to control Christians?

   ____

   ____

   ____

Chapter 11

The Truth That Will Set You Free

Nevertheless knowing that a man is not justified by the works of the Law but through faith in Christ Jesus, even we have believed in Christ Jesus, that we may be justified by faith in Christ, and not by the works of the law; since by the works of the Law shall no flesh be justified. (Galatians 3:16)

Most evangelicals would agree we are saved by grace through faith, and not by anything we have done or can do. A few add just a little "leaven" to "the lump of dough" (Galatians 5:9), such as the necessity of water baptism for salvation, wear this—don't wear that—and other outward observances. These things are relatively easy to see as "law," but there is a much more subtle perversion of truth that Satan uses to corrupt the purity of the gospel with. He uses subtle lies that draw us back to self-effort rather than resting in the finished work of Christ.

Not only are we saved by grace, "God's unmerited favor," we are also kept by grace, "God's ability for our inability." We receive the blessing of God by grace—getting what we don't deserve. As soon as we think we can earn God's favor, we have *fallen from grace.*

> You have been severed[8] from Christ, you who are
> seeking to be justified by law; you have fallen from
> grace. (Galatians 5:4)

To aid our understanding of this important truth, we need to define modern-day "law." We are no longer under Mosaic Law because "the law of the Spirit of life in Christ Jesus has set you free from the law of sin and death" (Romans 8:2).

When we receive God's gift of eternal life (which is Christ's life), we are immersed into Jesus. All that Jesus is—righteous, fully accepted by God the Father, unconditionally loved by God, ad infinitum—is ours as a free gift.

> He made Him who knew no sin to be sin on our
> behalf, that we might become the righteousness of
> God in Him. (II Corinthians 5:21)

Jesus did not abolish the law, but He fulfilled it. He lived a sinless life, took us to the cross with Him to free us from the jurisdiction of the law, and then gave us His life (Romans 6:4).

> For while we were in the flesh, the sinful passions,
> which were aroused by the Law, were at work in the
> members of our body to bear fruit for death. But now
> we have been released from the Law, having died to
> that by which we were bound, so that we serve in
> newness of the Spirit and not in oldness of the letter.
> (Romans 7:5–6)

---

[8] "Severed" does not refer to our salvation, but to the fact that Christ's life only flows through us when we are walking according to the Spirit. When we operate out of self-effort, we are walking according to the flesh, and the grace of God—"the power and desire to do God's will"—is not in operation at that moment. We could also think of a branch, if severed from a vine, would functionally be cut off from its source of life.

Since His sinless life, or nature, was given to us, we stand before God just as if we had never sinned; that is "justification."

> Nevertheless, knowing that a man is not justified by the works of the Law but through faith in Christ Jesus, even we have believed in Christ Jesus, that we may be justified by faith in Christ, and not by the works of the Law; since by the works of the Law shall no flesh be justified. (Galatians 2:16)

If we understand that in Christ, we are eternally *justified*, we can get off the religious treadmill and breathe a deep sigh of relief. Modern-day law then is anything we do to earn God's acceptance, love, or blessing. It is not the outward act, such as fasting, prayer, Bible study, giving, or a godly lifestyle that makes a practice the observance of law, but the motive of our hearts. Why do we do the things we do? If it is to get something from God or "to not get struck by lightning," we are observing our own version of the law. When we do this, we have severed ourselves from the grace of God and have traded the righteousness of Christ for self-righteousness. All our godly disciplines must flow from love for the Lord, not out of fear or self-centeredness.

What are the dangers of self-righteousness? One of the most hazardous results of self-righteousness is pride. It was pride that caused Satan's downfall, as he proclaimed he would become like the Most High God and was cast out of heaven.

> God is opposed to the proud, but gives grace to the humble. (I Peter 5:5b)

If the enemy of our souls can get us to become self-dependent, we will be walking "according to the flesh" (Romans 8:4b), and the grace of God, which is the power of God, will be successfully cut off from our lives in the areas of our self-sufficiency. Satan is then able to steal from us part of what he lost when he was cast from heaven. Satan "comes only to steal" from, "kill, and destroy" (John 10:10a),

God's creation in retaliation of all he lost through pride. If he can tempt us to follow our flesh in pride and self-dependence, then he wins that battle. "But thanks be to God, who gives us the victory through our Lord Jesus Christ" (I Corinthians 15:57), if we walk "according to the Spirit" (Romans 8:4b), God gives us the victory; but in our own wisdom and strength, we are destined to fail.

Again, Satan is extremely crafty and knows we would not fall for anything obvious, so he even uses religious activity to get our eyes off complete dependence on Christ's life within us. He wants us to depend on anything but Christ alone, our knowledge of scripture and our years of walking with the Lord or on the manifest presence of God in our ministry. Even our ministry itself can be become the object of our focus rather than Christ Himself. No matter how good or noble a discipline is, if we think we are successful in our Christian walk because of the "excellence" we have arrived at in any discipline, we have replaced "the simplicity and purity of devotion to Christ" (II Corinthians 11:3b), with the letter of the law. Remember, New Testament law is anything we do to earn God's acceptance, love, or blessing, rather than resting on the finished work of Christ.

> For neither is circumcision anything, nor uncircumcision, but a new creation. And those who will walk by this rule, peace and mercy be upon them, and upon the Israel of God. (Galatians 6:15–16)

Circumcision is representative of what the law said a man had to do to be right with God. The Apostle Paul is plainly telling the Galatians, it is not what they do or don't do that matters but the new creation within them. If they would live by the rule of "it is no longer I who live, but Christ lives in me" (Galatians 2:20), they would experience "peace and mercy" in their lives.

The next problem that arises out of self-righteousness is the expectation of wages due.

> But when the fullness of the time came, God sent forth His Son, born of a woman, born under the law,

in order that He might redeem those who were under
the Law, that we might receive the adoption as sons.
(Romans 4:4–5)

When we feel we deserve the favor of God because of what we have done for Him, then we insist upon what we believe we have coming. (Think of the pathetic picture of an ant demanding wages for service to a human being.) In our demanding, we become angry and disillusioned for not getting what we think we deserve. We also become ungrateful when what we receive is not as good as what we think we have earned. We become jealous when someone whose performance is not nearly as good as ours receives what we consider better or more than what we receive. Jesus points this out in Matthew chapter 20. Since "all of our righteousness is as filthy rags" (Isaiah 64:6), then we all would deserve hell no matter how good we have been. It is only by God's grace that we receive anything else. If we can get a true glimpse of our total unworthiness apart from Christ, we can start to become overwhelmingly grateful for all we will ever receive.

Self-righteousness, which again is any attitude other than complete dependence on the finished work of Christ, breeds pride and ungratefulness, and "stone throwing." Stone throwing is "seeing the speck that is in your brother's eye" but missing "the log in your own" (Matthew 7:3). Stone throwing is the absence of Christ's love and mercy. To the one who shows no mercy, none will be given. Jesus used the above example while talking to the Pharisees, since they exemplified self-righteousness. Jesus was trying to show them their spiritual blindness and their hard hearts. When we see our righteousness as a result of our keeping the list of rules we embrace, or as a result of our dedicated Christian service, then we "cast stones" (mental thoughts and verbal slander), at those who do not measure up like we do. Instead of giving the more unseemly members of the body more honor, more prayer, and more grace and mercy; we criticize, judge, and destroy those whom Jesus died for. Instead of embracing all those who are in Christ Jesus as members of His body, we separate ourselves, teach our children to look down on other denominations, and cast stones at their differences. This is not the heart of our Father. It is the product of the fleshly fruit of self-righteousness.

One last fruit of self-righteousness is condemnation. We have seen the condemnation that pride and stone throwing cause us to heap on each other, but there is another type of condemnation and that is the self-condemnation that observance of the law brings upon ourselves. When we measure our acceptance or "current standing" with God by our performance of what "our law" states is godly, then when our thoughts, behavior, and accomplishments do not measure very high on our scale, we feel unworthy and useless in God's kingdom. Our feeling of being frowned upon by God then causes us to hide in the bushes sewing fig leaves together to cover our feeling of nakedness and shame.

When Adam and Eve ate of the Tree of the Knowledge of Good and Evil, their eyes were opened to the fact of how sinful they were apart from complete dependence on God. As soon as their eyes turned to themselves instead of God, they felt naked and hid from Him. We must remember Adam was accustomed to walking with the Lord in the cool of the evening, and before eating of the forbidden tree, he had not felt ashamed. It was only after Adam's eyes were opened to the reality of how far short his "doing" was to the standard of God that he felt condemnation and shame. Before partaking of the fruit, Adam had no concept of right or wrong and consequently was without sin.

> For the Law brings about wrath,[9] but where there is
> no law, neither is there violation. (Romans 4:15)

> For until the Law, sin was in the world; but sin is not
> imputed when there is no law. (Romans 5:13)

------

[9] The word "wrath" comes from the original word, *orge*, which originally meant any natural impulse or desire, or disposition; it came to signify anger that is the strongest of all passions (Vine's Expository Dictionary).

Before the fall, sin was not imputed to Adam, so there was nothing to be ashamed of. When we realize we are without sin in God's eyes (we have become the righteousness of God in Christ Jesus), we will once again have nothing to be ashamed of and condemnation will have lost its hold. As long as we look to ourselves and our performance as a basis for our righteousness, we will always fall short and never feel worthy.

> For all have sinned and fall short of the glory of God, being justified as a gift by His grace through the redemption which is in Christ Jesus. (Romans 3:23,24)

> For we maintain that a man is justified by faith apart from works of the law. (Romans 3:28)

The great danger, of condemnation, is that we run from our only source of deliverance. When we realize that our performance falls short of God's holy standard, our only hope is to:

> Draw near with confidence to the throne of grace, that we may receive mercy and grace to help in time of need. (Hebrews 4:16)

When we humbly acknowledge that we do not have what it takes, we are a candidate for "God's ability for our inability," which is grace. When we run boldly to the throne of grace, "the Lord will accomplish what concerns" us (Psalm 138:8). He will strengthen us from within by His Spirit who lives in us. We are changed, by looking to Jesus, believing that the power of His life will make us like Him.

> But we all, with unveiled face beholding as in a mirror the glory of the Lord, are being transformed into the same image from glory to glory, just as from as from the Lord, the Spirit. (II Corinthians 3:18)

On the other hand, if we are depending on our own strength, our own capabilities, or even our spiritual gifts to make us acceptable in God's eyes, or in order to do His work, we will feel condemned when we do not succeed. We then become hypocrites to hide the lack of Christlikeness that is really in us and burn out serving God in the strength of the flesh.

The majority of the body of Christ is stuck, going around in circles in the "Wilderness of Sin," because of self-reliance. They will never enter the promised land of abundant life because of unbelief. In order to escape self-righteousness and the tyranny of the law, we must have "ceased from our own works" (Hebrews 4:10 KJV) and have rested in the One who fulfilled all the demands of the law for us. As soon as the revelation of being "freed from sin" (Romans 6:7) becomes real in our spirits, the law will no longer have dominion over us, and we will be freed from guilt and shame.

> For sin shall not be master over you, for you are not under the law but under grace. (Romans 6:14)

> There is therefore now no condemnation for those who are in Christ Jesus. (Romans 8:1)

In order for you to have the revelation of being "freed from sin," you need to have your mind renewed by scripture. Sin has nothing to do with the righteousness of a believer in Christ.

> For Christ did not enter a holy place made with hands, a mere copy of the true one, but into heaven itself, now to appear in the presence of God for us; nor was it that He should offer Himself often, as the high priest enters the holy place year by year with blood not his own. Otherwise, He would have needed to suffer often since the foundation of the world; but now once at the consummation He has been manifested to put away sin by the sacrifice of Himself. And inasmuch as it is appointed for men to die once, and

> after this comes judgment; so Christ also, having been
> offered once to bear the sins of many, shall appear a
> second time for salvation without reference to sin, to
> those who eagerly await Him. (Hebrews 9:24–28)

The words "put away," in verse 26, come from the original word, *athethesis*, which *Vine's Expository Dictionary* defines as "to abolish or disannul." Jesus disannulled sin by the sacrifice of Himself. In other words, our sin is voided by His sacrifice.

> Blessed is the man whose sin the Lord will not take
> into account. (Romans 4:8)

How many times does Christ have to offer Himself? Verse 25 of Hebrews chapter 9 states that the sacrifice was offered once. Jesus will not die again for the sins we commit tomorrow. Neither does the confession of tomorrow's sins apply the blood of Jesus to them. The exchange of His nature for ours, at the time of our salvation, gave us His righteousness. Our performance determines what we reap, not our standing before God.

> For the one who sows to his own flesh shall from the
> flesh reap corruption, but the one who sows to the Spirit
> shall from the Spirit reap eternal life. (Galatians 6:8)

> (Eternal life is Christ's life, or abundant life, which we
> experience when He is ruling our hearts.)

Refer again to Hebrews 9:28. The next time Christ appears, it will be "without reference to sin." The sin issue was dealt with at the cross and is no longer an issue to those who "eagerly await Him." Sin has nothing to do with the righteousness of a believer in Christ!

> I do not nullify the grace of God; for if righteousness
> comes through the Law, then Christ died needlessly.
> (Galatians 2:21)

> The sting of death is sin, and the power of sin is the law; but thanks be to God who gives us the victory through our Lord Jesus Christ. (I Corinthians 15:56)

Where law is applied, sin is fueled. Where law is applied, we put ourselves under the power of sin that Christ set us free from. The common argument against grace is the fear of what people will do if they have no rules to keep them in check. That may be good rational thinking, but it is not scriptural. Rules have never kept the flesh under control. In fact, the opposite is true. If you tell your flesh it can't have or do something, it immediately craves what you have forbidden. If you have ever been on a diet, you will understand this principle. The flesh cannot be controlled, reformed, or modified. It can only be crucified, by agreeing with scripture that the power of the risen Christ has taken its place. Take your place of death with Christ and "rest" in His life!

Personal Study

1. What do you personally believe you would have to do to lose your salvation?

   ____

   ____

   ____

2. What does the phrase "fallen from grace" refer to in Galatians 5:4?

   ____

   ____

   ____

3. What is the definition of "modern-day law"?

   ____

   ____

   ____

4. What are four fruits of self-righteousness?

   ____

   ____

   ____

5. How are we changed into the image of Christ?

   ____

   ____

   ____

6. How will the sins you commit from today onward affect your righteousness?

   ____

   ____

   ____

7. How does your performance affect your life on earth?

____

____

____

8. What effect does the application of "law" have on the flesh?

____

____

____

CHAPTER 12

Let the Peace of God Rule Your Heart

You should now understand the power of God that is available to you through His life that lives in you. You should also understand the need of coming to the end of your own resources, to complete dependence on Christ as your source. Christ is your new life. All you need for life and godliness is in you at new birth. The power of sin is cut off, and the battle you face is only the unrenewed part of your mind, will, and emotions fighting against the change in command. The remaining question then is, how do we know when we are prompted by the flesh and when we are being led by the Spirit? The barometer that God has given us is His peace. We are to let the "peace of Christ rule in our hearts." (Colossians 3:13).

In the last chapter, we studied the futility of performance-based acceptance. One of the scriptures we looked at was Galatians 6:15–16:

> For neither is circumcision anything, nor uncircumcision, but a new creation. And those who will walk by this rule, peace and mercy be upon them, and upon the Israel of God.

Not only do these two verses stress the importance of the need to concentrate on "Christ in you," rather than on your performance, they also promise peace to those who walk according to this rule. In other words, when we acknowledge that our old nature is dead and Christ is our new nature, and when we are totally dependent on His life for all things, we will have peace. The peace we experience when we quit trying to please God and men is the guide for our continued walk in Him. The greatest level of peace we have ever walked in will deepen as we continue to be conformed to the image of Christ. Consequently, our level of peace will also be a measurement of our spiritual maturity.

> And the work of righteousness will be peace, and the service of righteousness, quietness and confidence forever. (Isaiah 32:17)

"The work of righteousness" in this verse is not what we do for God, but what God does in us. "The work of righteousness" is what happens to an individual who is allowing the righteous nature of Christ, which was received at new birth, to permeate their mortal body. When the life of Christ flows through the mind, will, and emotions, they are changed into His likeness. One result of dependence on the righteousness of Christ is peace. The long-term effect of walking through this life, dependent on His life, will be quietness in our spirit and a confidence in His ability. This quietness and confidence will keep us calm in the midst of any storm.

Jesus has compared Himself to the peace in the middle of a storm. Just as a tornado roars in funnel formation, there is an eye in the center of the violent winds that is perfectly calm. Life can be like a tornado. There are winds of adversity that seem to tear apart all we hold dear, but in the midst of it all, we can walk in peace, because Jesus is the calm in the midst of the storm. If we train ourselves to hide in Him, we can remain peaceful no matter what is going on around us. Conversely, if we allow our minds to be filled with data from adverse circumstances around us, our emotions will begin to react, and we can quickly loose our peace. Tormenting thoughts, such as "We don't have enough money to pay our bills," "My spouse is going to leave me," or "My spouse will never change," can quickly suck us from the peace "which surpasses all comprehension" (Philippians 4:7) in the center of the storm, to feelings of hopelessness and helplessness.

Fear is believing that what you think or perceive with your senses is more real than what God has promised to work in and through you. If we focus our minds on His ability in us, fear will have no place of access.

> If God is for us, who is against us? He who did not spare His own Son, but delivered Him up for us all, how will He not also with Him freely give us all things? (Romans 8:31b,32)

Peace is a fruit of the Spirit, when we walk according to the Spirit (with the Spirit in control), we will be at peace. When the flesh is in control, there may be a fleshly counterfeit of peace, but the real thing will not be present. The longer you practice letting the peace of Christ rule your heart, the easier it becomes. Meanwhile, don't be any harder on yourself than God is on you. Since He knows the frailty of our humanity, He is not the least bit surprised when we "flesh out." In fact, Jesus through His death and resurrection became the all-sufficient provision for our weakness. He assured the Apostle Paul, "My grace is sufficient for you, for power is perfected in weakness" (II Corinthians 12:9).

Ask the Lord for His grace to learn to walk out of the Life within you, rather than by your list of rules designed to control your flesh. When I first determined to do this, I told the Lord that if I was prompted in my spirit to do something and it wouldn't do any harm (not counting harm to my reputation, which I had already given to Him), I would go for it. I am sure I did some unnecessary things during that training period, but I fine-tuned my response to His life within me. When I have complete peace about an action, I go in that direction. If there is hesitation in my spirit, then I stop until I know why not proceeding until there is a peaceful alternative. For most decisions of life, you will not feel specific prompting in your spirit. Continue on with the last directions the Lord has given you and the responsibilities of your everyday life, unless you feel a hesitation in your spirit. When you feel a hesitation, sometimes called a "check," find out why before proceeding.

As you walk the exchanged life, you will begin to know the difference between the hesitations of the flesh and the hesitation of the spirit. You will also learn to recognize the way your particular flesh responds in certain situations, which we will call your "flesh pattern." Let's use, for example, a person who has always been afraid to speak in front of people; we will call our person Bill. Bill is asked by his pastor to lead the Bible study on Wednesday night. Bill asks to pray about this opportunity before he gives his answer. As he prays, he feels unsettled inside and has trouble determining the Lord's leading. One thing Bill must take into account is his flesh pattern. His flesh has always feared speaking in front of people, so his uneasy feeling could very well be the emotions of his flesh. Bill's spirit could actually be at complete peace, maybe even excited about the opportunity, while his flesh—at the same time—could be full of fear.

In a case like Bill's, it would be wise to ask one or two close friends to also pray about the opportunity presented. Whenever we are faced with a decision we know will tempt or upset our flesh, it may be wise to counsel with others. It will take some time of practicing being led by the spirit, before it will be safe to "trust you heart" in an area of personal prejudice. Eventually, you will begin to know your "flesh pattern" and know the difference between the prompting of your flesh and your spirit.

I will use myself as another example of fleshly prejudice. I do not like being without transportation. Calling me a "free spirit" could be an understatement. Consequently, I know that I will have to guard my heart carefully if my car breaks down and my source of transportation is cut off. Since we live quite a distance from any town, I could be ready to use almost any method of obtaining transportation, including buying the first car anywhere close to our requirements—just give me my wheels back! Knowing my flesh pattern, I am careful of the nature of my input in our transportation decisions. The peace I could feel in my heart could just be my flesh's counterfeit at getting what it wants. Whenever our flesh is gratified, it can give a false sense of peace. Be careful—know yourself and be honest with yourself.

Don't let these warnings scare you. The law doesn't give you the power to overcome, so you are going to have to grow up in the Lord and trust your heart. Remember, you have a new heart, which was created to do good. The prophet Ezekiel spoke prophetically of what would happen at new birth.

> Moreover, I will give you a new heart and put a new spirit within you, and I will remove the heart of stone from your flesh and give you a heart of flesh. And I will put My Spirit within you and cause you to walk in My statutes, and you will be careful to observe My ordinances. (Ezekiel 36:26,27)

Paul to the Church at Ephesus again declared the provision God made for a holy walk.

> For we are His workmanship, created in Christ Jesus for good works, which God prepared beforehand, that we should walk in them. (Ephesians 2:10)

We have to remember:

> That it is God who is at work in us, operating both the power and desire, to will and to work for His good pleasure. (Philippians 2:13 (AMP))

God is the one who drew us to Himself through His Spirit. He then placed His life in us through the death of His Son. He continues to work out what He placed within us by His Spirit. We can choose, by our free will, to run our own lives. However, if we desire to do His will, we must trust Him to lead us.

> Delight yourself in the Lord; and He will give you the desires of your heart. Commit your way to the Lord, Trust also in Him, and He will do it. (Psalm 37:4,5)

> The steps of a man are established by the Lord, And He delights in his way. When he falls, he shall not be

> hurled headlong; Because the Lord is the One who
> holds his hand. (Psalm 37:23,24)

> Trust in the LORD with all your heart, And lean
> not on your own understanding; In all your ways
> acknowledge Him, And He shall direct your paths.
> (Proverbs 3:5,6 (NKJV))

God is much more involved in each and every detail of your everyday life than you could ever imagine. It is remarkable how He arranges "divine appointments," protects us, and gently leads us to His expected end, when we aren't even aware of His leading. Let His peace rule your heart. He will take care of the rest.

> For I know the plans that I have for you, declares the
> LORD, plans for welfare and not for calamity to give
> you a future and a hope. (Jeremiah 29:11)

The longer we walk dependent on the Life within us, the more we will know His prompting and the more we will know His peace. The more we read His word, the more we will know Him, for He is the Living Word. As we spend time communing with Him daily, His will and His ways will become more familiar.

> For everyone who partakes only of milk is not accus-
> tomed to the word of righteousness, for he is a babe.
> But solid food is for the mature, who because of prac-
> tice have their senses trained to discern good and evil.
> (Hebrews 5:13,14)

Eventually, we will know Him intimately. We will know what grieves Him and what gives Him joy. His emotions will start to be ours, His will—our will. When He takes this place in our hearts, we will feel more secure in letting His peace rule our hearts—trusting His life to lead us and His love to keep us.

Personal Study

1.   Write out the definition of "fear" given in this chapter.

   ____

   ____

   ____

2.   Write out II Corinthians 12:9.

   ____

   ____

   ____

3.   List several ways that your "flesh" habitually responds in certain situations. This is your "flesh pattern."

   ____

   ____

   ____

4.   Name an area or situation that you know would not be wise for you to make an important decision in by yourself, because of your flesh's propensity.

   ____

   ____

   ____

5.   Why are you afraid to trust your heart? What does scripture have to say about this?

   ____

   ____

   ____

The Way of the Lord

> Stand by the way and see and ask for the ancient
> paths, where the good way is, and walk in it; and you
> shall find rest for your souls. But they said, we will
> not walk in it. And I set watchmen over you, saying,
> Listen to the sound of the trumpet! But they said,
> "We will not listen." (Jeremiah 6:16–17)

Ever since the Garden of Eden, God has been giving His creation—mankind—a chance to choose dependence on Him or to go their own way. When Adam and Eve chose to eat of the fruit of the Tree of Knowledge of Good and Evil, they rejected God's plan for their lives. Whenever we choose our way, the result is a decrease in the quality of life, which leads to destruction. Galatians 6:8 calls it *corruption.*

> For the one who sows to his own flesh shall from the
> flesh reap corruption, but the one who sows to the Spirit
> shall from the Spirit reap eternal life. (Galatians 6:8)

Vine's Expository Dictionary defines *corruption* in this text as: "being brought into an inferior or worse condition." This is the opposite of Christ's life, which is abundant life. Whenever we live independent of God, we are sowing to the flesh, whether the action seems "good" or not.

> Not that we are adequate in ourselves to consider any-
> thing as coming from ourselves, but our adequacy is
> from God, who also made us adequate as servants of
> a new covenant, not of the letter but of the Spirit;
> for the letter kills, but the Spirit gives life. But if the
> ministry of death, in letters engraved on stones, came
> with glory, so that the sons of Israel could not look
> intently at the face of Moses because of the glory of
> his face, fading as it was, how will the ministry of
> the Spirit fail to be even more with glory? For if the
> ministry of condemnation has glory, much more does
> the ministry of righteousness abound in glory. (II
> Corinthians 3:5–9)

There may be a certain amount of glory, of harvest, or seeming blessing from our "good works" according to the flesh, but it is still a "ministry of death" (II Corinthians 3:7). There is only life or death—nothing in between. What comes forth from our own natural ability is from the flesh, which is death. Life can only come from Christ, for He is the Life.

> Jesus said to him, "I am the way, and the truth, and
> the life: no one comes to the Father, but through Me."
> (John 14:6)

> For the bread of God is that which comes down out
> of heaven, and gives life to the world. (John 6:33)

> You search the Scriptures, because you think that in
> them you have eternal life; and it is these that bear
> witness of Me; and you are unwilling to come to Me,
> that you may have life. (John 5:39,40)

His life flows to this world through us. Only when we are totally dependent on Him to live His life through us, is our ministry of the Spirit. Only then does it bring the glory of eternal life.

God continues to give us choices, day after day, hour by hour, to choose dependence on Him. As we choose "the way of the Lord" (Proverbs 10:29), we will be conformed to the image of Christ. Each time we choose to walk according to the Spirit, a little more of our flesh is renewed and the easier it is to yield to the Spirit.

God's purpose is not only to prepare us to rule and reign with Him, but to conform us to the image of His Son to such a degree that our life is a revelation of the life of Christ within us to a world that does not know Him. Our Father's purpose is for our eyes to be so fixed on our bridegroom that we do not notice the stormy blasts of the temporal. There is a place "hidden with Christ in God" (Colossians 3:3), where Christ's love for us and our love for Him will hide the inequities of this life, for "love covers a multitude of sins" (I Peter 4:8).

Our loving Father has an eternal plan laid out for each of us, even as an engineer lays out the tracks for a railway. He is the divine engineer, and we only need to follow Him. The route is so rough at times we could be tempted to think the engineer doesn't know what He is doing, but He makes no mistakes. Even when we stray, if we repent of running our own lives, He is able to get us back on track. God is sovereign, He is all-powerful, and He has all knowledge; yet this God who is beyond our comprehension loves each one of us, just as if we were His only child. In his love, He allows trials to custom make us into trophies of His grace. There is nothing that has ever happened to us—no matter how horrific—that God is not able to work together for our good (Romans 8:28).

So be encouraged! For even though we will have tribulation in this world (John 16:33), Jesus overcame the world. This is great news for a Christian. Since Jesus lives in us, the same power that raised Jesus from the dead can be the life source for every child of God—but the choice is yours!

APPENDIX I

Zoe vs. Bios

In the Bible, two Greek words translated as "life" are *zoe* and *bios*. A short study of these two words will help you understand the life that Christ gives us at new birth.

Just as when we were born the first time, we received the life of our parents. When we were born the second time, of the Spirit, we received the life of our Heavenly Father, through His Son Jesus. *Zoe* is the kind of life God has, which became our life when we received Jesus as Savior. As we have previously discussed, Christ's life is synonymous with eternal life. Now we may add that *zoe* is a description of Christ's life, as well as eternal life.

Zoe is not an extension of days and activities, nor a measurement of time and space, but a description of the *quality* of God's life. On the other hand, *bios* speaks of the duration of our life on earth, of our manner of life, or the means of life. *Bios* is a description of our existence on this earth.

When Adam sinned in the garden, he died spiritually. That means *zoe* (the kind of life God has) left him. When *zoe* left Adam and Eve, a void remained where life had once been. In an effort to fill the void, mankind developed a lifestyle of self-fulfillment. The systems of self-fulfillment, such as religion, relationships, education, occupation, hobbies, etc. developed a counterfeit life of human flesh in an attempt to regain what was lost. This is *bios*.

Scriptural references for *zoe* include:
John 14:6
I John 1:1–2
John 1:4
John 3:15–16
John 3:36
John 11:25–26
John 4:14
John 6:35
John 8:12
John 5:39–40

Scriptural references for *bios* include:
I Timothy 2:2
II Timothy 2:4
Luke 8:14
I John 2:16
Mark 12:44
I Peter 4:3

APPENDIX II

My Action Plan to Forgive

The initials of the person I choose to forgive _______________.

In the space provided below, list the injustices for which you need to forgive this person. Number each injustice with the appropriate code from the list that follows. In the lower section of this page, list the ways you have responded to this person in the past. Use an asterisk to indicate those responses for which you need to apologize. Also list what you should do next and the date by which you will do it.

Injustices I need to forgive: Present Status

____

____

____

____

____

____

____

(0)   I still feel resentment and a desire to retaliate.

(1)   I have a barrier toward God because I have not forgiven.

(2)   I have made a decision to quit hurting the other person.

(3)   I am willing to be made willing to apologize and forgive.

(4)   I am finding that I want to apologize and forgive.

(5)   I am trying to determine if I should talk about this with the other person.

(6)   I have apologized and am making restitution where necessary.

(7)   I am calling others' offenses, and my wrong response, the same as God calls it, "sin."

(8)   I have forgiven the person based on Jesus blood payment, similar to how He has paid for my sin.

(9)   I am open to dealing with any offenses I have held against God.

(10)   I am doing the hard work of forgiving myself.

(11)   I am praying that my memories will be healed by God.

(12)   I am working on guarding my thoughts and now keeping the issue closed.

(13)   I am willing to temporarily experience the consequences of sin, until God redeems them for me.

(14)   I am learning, where necessary, how to set barriers to minimize future hurt.

P – Add a "P" in front of the number if you are praying about the situation the number represents.

T – Add a "T" in front of the number if you are talking with a reliable friend about it.

Ways I have responded in the past and those responses for which I need to apologize:

____

____

____

____

____

____

____

What I should do next: Target Date:

____

____

____

____

____

____

____

Adapted with permission – Ken Geelhoed, 2007.

About the Author

Rhonda J. Mead is an ordained minister, Christian writer, and speaker. Her passion for over 30 years has been sharing and teaching biblical principles for personal freedom and an overcoming life through the power of the cross. Rhonda appeared on the TCT Network's Ask the Pastor program for over 19 years, as well as on her locally produced program, Rhonda From the Heart.

Rhonda, along with her husband Richard, serve as co-directors of New Life Outreach, a nonprofit ministry based out of Holton, MI. It is through this global outreach that Rhonda and Richard work to share the message of personal and regional transformation through the power of the cross.